Bill Idelson's Writing Class

a scriptwriting curriculum

By: Bill Idelson

Edited By: Steve Atinsky

PUBLISHED IN THE USA BY:

BearManor Media
PO Box 71426
Albany, GA 31708
www.BearManorMedia.com

ISBN 978-1-59393-100-1

Printed in the United States.

Reprint edition copy edited by Lon Davis.

Cover design and layout by Howie Idelson.

Interior design and layout by Valerie Thompson.

TABLE OF CONTENTS

To all my students, past and present.

FOREWORD

You know how there are people that you meet who actually change your life? Well, for me, Bill Idelson was not one of those people. He didn't change my life. He gave me a life. Before I met him, I was an aspiring writer (aspiring meaning unsuccessful) and I had been living in LA for a while. I can't say exactly how long because I'd gotten into the habit of lying about it and now I really can't remember. I didn't know much at the time but I did know that "I just moved to LA and I have nothing going on" sounded a lot better than "I've been in LA for four years and have nothing going on."

But it's not like I hadn't tried. When I first moved here I submitted my *Cheers* spec script to the Warner Bros. New Writers workshop. A month later, I had an interview with them. I remember thinking, "Wow, becoming a television writer is going to be a lot easier than I thought it would be. I mean, I figured I'd have to struggle for at least a few months . . ." They didn't let me in.

Many years later, when the show I created, *The War At Home*, was picked up as a series, I received a phone call from Peter Roth, the head of my studio which happens to be Warner Bros.

"Congratulations, Rob," he said.

"Thank you, Peter. You know I was extremely disappointed when I didn't get into the Warner Bros. New Writers program fourteen years ago. But I think I can finally let that go now."

Anyway, there was a lot of disappointment in those early years for me. Contacts that didn't wind up helping me like I'd hoped they would. Agents that didn't return calls. Agents that did return calls and told me they didn't like my writing.

A lot of people ask me the secret to my success and I always say, "I didn't give up." And I never did. Probably because at the time I was a big pothead. Before waking up one day and getting the idea that I would be a television writer, I had never wanted to do or be anything. The fact that years had gone by without a hint of a paycheck never deterred me from my goal. I'd just smoke another joint and say . . . "It'll happen."

But I didn't just sit around getting high. Through it all, I kept on writing. Mostly mediocre scripts. And the thing is, I kind of knew that my writing wasn't that great but I didn't know how to make it better. So I took classes. I mean, that's how you learn, right? Wrong. I took several classes at UCLA. Some of the teachers had credits on shows that I had watched. And they were really nice. And they all said I was funny and took an interest in me. What they didn't do, was tell me how to write a better script.

One day, a friend I met in one of these classes told me that he was going to a free introductory class by a writing teacher that taught out of his house. He said he sounded really cool and had written on a lot of shows . . . *M*A*S*H, Happy Days, Andy Griffith, Get Smart, Bob Newhart.* Well, those were some of my favorite shows of all time and it was free and I wasn't doing anything that day (Who am I kidding? I wasn't doing anything *any* day) and I decided to check it out. My friend didn't show up for some reason and decided not to take the class. I think he eventually moved back to New Jersey and went to work at his father's accounting firm. He may or may not have eventually killed himself. That's not important. What is important is that I did show up and that was the day that I first met Bill Idelson.

Now, knowing what Bill taught me about writing—like *get the story started quickly*—I should probably go back and cut the first five or six paragraphs. They really are off-story and not that funny. But screw it, he wanted an introduction to his book, he'll take what he gets.

Five minutes into the introductory class, I knew that something very different was going on here. Bill asked the group of would-be writers who came that day, "What is a story?" Some girl raised her hand and gave some long-winded generic answer. Bill growled at her that she was an idiot and didn't know the first thing about writing. She burst into tears and ran out of the house. I had seen enough. I immediately wrote Bill a check and signed up for the class.

And here's the thing: I didn't know what a story was either. I was also an idiot who didn't know the first thing about writing. And it occurred to me, maybe this was the reason I hadn't gotten an agent and didn't have a job writing on a sitcom. But unlike the other idiot who left crying that day, I listened to every word Bill said. And I kept coming back.

Week after week, we'd have different writing assignments and I worked harder on these scenes than I ever did on anything in my entire life. And every week, when my scene would be read Bill would say, "That stinks." And then he'd explain why. And that was the difference between this class and all the others I'd taken. And all the books I'd read. See, here's the thing: Some people are good writers; some people are good teachers. But Bill happens to be both. And what he teaches is how to be a professional writer. What is a professional writer? Someone who makes a living at it. So much of what we did around the table in Bill's class was practice for what goes on at the table in the writers' room. Breaking a story, giving notes, re-breaking a story, taking notes, learning how to take criticism, and endless rewriting. Bill once said (and it's so true), "If you don't want input and you don't want to make changes to your writing, then you should be a poet. No one ever has notes for a poet. Unfortuately, poets don't make a very good living."

After taking Bill's class, I had learned the building blocks of writing. My writing was getting better. Maybe even *good*. But still, I had no agent, no job. Bill suggested I *get a partner*. Partners get hired more than people on their own because the producer gets two for the price of one. So if you really want to work, get a partner. If you want to work a lot, get a partner who's a *woman*. If you want to work forever, get a partner who's a *black* woman.

At the time, Bill had an ongoing workshop for people who had taken his class. We'd bring in things we were working on and it was a place to have it read aloud and to get feedback from the other writers and, more importantly, Bill, who always seemed to have a fix for whatever problem you had. It was at one of those workshops that I first met Ellen. She had taken Bill's class. She was funny, smart, pretty—and she was an actress and a brilliant improviser. She was also Bill's daughter. I figured: Now *there's* someone who would be a *great* partner . . .

And she was for over ten years. We started on the Emmy award-winning HBO show, *Dream On* and never stopped. We worked on *Caroline in the City, Ellen, Suddenly Susan, Will and Grace,* and a bunch of others. We even created and shot our own pilot for the WB network before Ellen got sick and passed away. One of the reasons she was such a good partner is that we had both taken Bill's class and we thought about things the same way. In fact, hardly a week went by when—we didn't refer back to something we had learned from Bill. Ellen used to joke that Bill wanted her to take his class because she was an actress and he wanted her to have something to fall back on. Only Bill could think of being a television writer as something to fall back on. But he was right. Maybe it was because he knew that he had taught her everything she needed to know to be a professional writer.

It's been a long time since I've taken Bill's class. Over the years, I've met and worked with a lot of writers who also took the class. They've all done really well. And I don't think it's a coincidence. As you read this book, you might be tempted to think, "Well maybe that's the way they did it on *The Bob Newhart Show* a million years ago. But what does this old fart know about what goes on now?" Let me be very clear about this . . . Whatever Bill says, he is right. About everything. Do what he says. I did. And I haven't done so bad.

ROB LOTTERSTEIN
CREATOR/EXECUTIVE PRODUCER
THE WAR AT HOME

PREFACE

You have enrolled in Bill Idelson's writing class and are now seated in Bill and Seemah's kitchen with other students at a pine table that once belonged to Humphrey Bogart and was bought at his estate auction in Beverly Hills.

You took the class because Bill's students are reputed to get jobs in television and movies more consistently than those who have come from other classes in the country.

Bill is now ready to begin the first session, and you will experience his course from beginning to end.

And the rest is up to you.

CLASS ONE
GETTING YOUR HEAD ON STRAIGHT

His success rate certainly says something. He doesn't teach that many people and a lot of people seem to be working.

—Ellen Plummer,
Co-Executive Producer,
Friends

O.K. There are a lot of writers out there. Millions, billions, maybe trill—. It staggers the imagination. Every semester, every college and university puts out a bunch of writers, and you can imagine how many upper-level schools there are. Most of the students who want to make a career out of it come to Hollywood because that's where it's at. A lot of them wind up in the Hollywood Hills—you know, where the sign is. They live alone, or with a roommate, a girlfriend, boyfriend, in an apartment or rented room . . . and they're writers. If you go to a party, you'll meet them. You ask them what they do and they're writers. Of course, at the moment they're working at Toys R Us, Best Buy, Starbucks, etc., but they're really writers. And they're all working on a script that's going to change their life. Usually it's a big project: a screenplay, a play, or a book. Novels are popular because they take a long time, maybe years, and it gives them a long while to be writers. The next time you see them, ask them what's happening, and they casually say, "Working on a novel," ask no more.

Now, you have this great horde, this army of writers . . .

(Bill spreads his hands over a wide expanse of the table.)

. . . and the sad thing is, ninety-nine percent of them will never make a nickel from writing. (Pause) Isn't that sad? It's sad.

Now . . .

(Bill puts the tips of his thumbs together and makes a tiny corral with his fingers.)

. . . down here there's a small group of writers who write the TV shows and movies that we see. They're the working writers. They can give the IRS an estimate of what they'll make next year. Two hundred thousand, five hundred thousand, maybe a million—and they do it.

(Long pause)

Now, what's your question? I'm sure you have a question.

There is another long pause. No one wants to appear foolish at this early stage. Finally, someone gets up his courage. "What's the difference between . . . ?"

Exactly. Good question. Do you think the people down here are smarter than all the people out here?

Someone else ventures a weak "No . . ."

I don't either. It's just that these people don't know what these other people know. Now, what do they know?

Another pause.

A wise-guy or girl tries a joke: "They know somebody who works at Universal." Gets a laugh.

Wrong. And I'll tell you why. The mantra in Hollywood is: I gotta save my ass. Now, if you got a brother-in-law who works at the studios, and he gives you a job to write a script, and it turns out to be a dud, he's just thrown away fifteen thousand of the company's money and endangered his ass. Do you think he's gonna jeopardize his two-hundred-thousand-a-year job to buy your script? Uh-uh. The same is true about screwing your way to the top. No one pays that much to get laid. I don't say it never happens, but the percentage is low.

No, the truth is, these guys down here know something the other guys don't. What is it?

(Shrugging of shoulders, rolling of eyes. Maybe a few more attempts at an answer.)

Want me to tell you, and save stress on your brain?

"Yes! Tell us!" (for Chrissake!)

They know it's a *business.*

(Silence, then derisive chuckles.)

Bill smiles. Yeah, it doesn't seem important, but it's *very* important. Have any of you had a job in a retail business? Selling stuff in a store, for instance? (A couple of hands go up.) What's the first rule of business?

Somebody says, kind of under their breath, "The customer is always right." Somebody else says, "Give 'em what they want."

Right! Right! The customer is king, no? You're in business. And if you're in the writing business, what's your script?

A pause. "Your product."

Exactly! Your script is your product. And in order to sell your product, what must your product do?

"Satisfy the customer."

Right! Now let's stipulate right here that people hate to take out their wallet and pay you money. For anything . . . *unless it satisfies their needs and desires.* Now, say your product is a breakfast cereal. You make breakfast cereal. And you know how when you're in a store, you go down the aisle and there's boxes and boxes of breakfast cereal? What is going to make them pay for *your* cereal?

People shrug, mystified. Finally, someone says:

"It tastes good? And . . ."

"Stop right there. It tastes good. Now, suppose you want to buy a refrigerator. You and your husband or wife, girlfriend or boyfriend, go into an appliance store and look at refrigerators. The first one you see is set up as a demonstrator. It's got food in it. But things don't look good. The lettuce is wilting, the ice cream is leaking down the side. The salesman says, "The guy that made this refrigerator really fulfilled himself. He got his rocks off. He thinks this refrigerator says something. It sends a message." What do you say to that?

A few mumbled answers.

Fuck 'm. Right?

(Laughter)

Sure, the refrigerator has to keep your food cold. You won't buy one that doesn't. It must satisfy *you*. Makes no difference what the maker thinks. Do you understand that?

(Nods)

O.K. Now what must *your* product have to induce the customer to buy it?

Timidly: "It has to be cold and taste good?"

(Lots of laughs)

No, no. The *cereal* has to taste good. The *refrigerator* needs to keep your food cold. The script has to have its own thing to make you buy it. Got it?

"Oh. Yeah, I see."

So what is it?

(Puzzlement)

"It has to be good?"

What does that mean?

"It has to be entertaining."

What does that mean?

"It has to make you laugh."

Uh-uh. Should I tell you?

"Yes, tell us!"

(Pause) It has to have a story.

(Pause, then incredulous giggles)

It almost seems too simple, doesn't it? But it's true. If you want to sell your product and make a lot of money, it's got to have a story. The people in the Hollywood Hills never learn that. What do *they* write?

(Shrugs)

I'll tell you. Clever dialogue. Stream of consciousness. Hip stuff. A trick ending. Things to inflate their ego. To impress the reader with how smart they are and how much they know. All things the reader doesn't care about, much less wants to pay for. The reader wants a story. So why don't they write stories?

(Pause) "It's too hard?"

Bingo! It's too hard. When you go to a movie or a play, or watch television, you've got to have a story. But that never seems to translate to people when they write. It's great to *watch* a story, but it's hard to *write* one. But the cardinal rule is . . . no story, no money. You need a story . . . that makes the juices flow. Do you know what I mean by that?

(Heads shake slowly)

Down here . . . Bill touches just below his chest. Something's got to stir . . .

"You've got to *feel* something."

Right! You got to feel amused, or sad, or frightened, horrified, disgusted, turned on . . . sexually.

That's what you want when you go to the theatre. But without a story you can't do that for the audience. You can't do anything. You've got to have a story first.

The faces around the table began showing signs of tiny bulbs going on in their brains.

Stories are fundamental to the human psyche and have been since the beginnings of man. If you go through the prehistoric caves where man first lived you see paintings on the walls. What are those paintings?

"Stories?"

Stories. Told by people who are compelled to describe what their life is like, to people who come after them. And what are those stories about?

"Wars, killing . . ."

Blood and guts. Sex and violence. Because that was the essence of their life. Stories that made the juices flow. I remember one . . . of a man shoving a spear down the throat of a lion. I'm sure that made the hunter's juices flow when it happened. And it made my juices flow when I saw it. In Pompeii there were pictures on the walls, painted before the volcano destroyed the city, of men and women having sex.

The truth is, people have got to have stories. Stories are as basic as food or sex. People cannot live without stories. During the Cold War a group of psychiatrists went to Russia to observe orphan babies who had been institutionalized. These babies were virtually warehoused. Very little human contact, no one to tell them stories. The psychiatrists found that the babies' brains showed signs of shrinkage. The human body needs exercise to stay in shape. So does the brain by exercising the imagination.

What is practically the first thing a toddler says when he learns to speak?

"'No!'" says a girl.

(Laughs)

Good answer, but not the one I'm looking for. It's 'Mommy, tell me a story.' And she can tell him the same story she told him the day before. Jack climbs the beanstalk to see the goose that lays the golden eggs. And the Giant comes along: 'Fee fie, fo fum, I smell the blood of an Englishman!' And the kid is happy. It made his juices flow yesterday and it did the same today. He doesn't need a new story or an original story. He doesn't even need a very clever story. It only needs to make the juices flow. Now, have a doughnut and some coffee and we'll talk further.

◆　❖　◆

We are in an airport lounge, where you wait to board a plane. People are doing what people do in such a place. They are reading the paper, looking at a magazine, talking to friends, passing time. Suddenly we are aware of an argument, over in the corner. Two men, speaking a foreign language, are in a heated discussion, and, intuitively, because we are all possessed of this kind of instinct, we know this is not a frivolous chat. Blood is in the air. What do we do?

"Leave!"

Well, maybe our first impulse is to get out of there. But there is something else operating with us: The necessity of appearing *cool*. The need to conform to the accepted code of conduct. If we jump up and run in a panic we certainly would not appear *cool*. We would look foolish and we can't have that.

So we sit there. The guy next to you reading the newspaper has read the same sentence half a dozen times and still doesn't know what it says. The other people, for the most part, do not turn and stare at the two men, but they are connected inexorably by ear. The people with kids make sure they know where they are.

Now the argument grows hotter. Now what do we do? The guy lowers his newspaper. People check for the exits. But no one moves. It wouldn't be *cool*. The juices are flowing faster. At this point, one of the combatants sounds conciliatory. We don't understand the words, but the tone leads us to believe there is a chance that violence can be averted. The guy next to you raises his newspaper and finds out what the sentence says. The heart rate drops. People relax.

Now one of the rivals pulls a knife! A murmur of fear goes through the seated crowd. If it had been a gun, people would have hit the floor, but a knife is dangerous only to an adversary. But still, a few people get to their feet, move toward the exit, their hearts pounding.

We can keep this tale going for a while, with the intensity of the hostility rising and falling, but it's served our purpose. What do we learn from it that is useful to a writer?

The students frown. "Everybody reacts differently?"

No, the opposite. Everyone reacts pretty much the same. It's called "group behavior," and is important to a writer. It's what makes hits and flops. If you watch an audience during an emotional scene, you'll see the handkerchiefs all come out at the same time. People are very much the same. They have the same sort of organs: heart, stomach, nerve endings, entrails, etc. It's what makes it possible to transfer a human heart to another human. It makes it possible to evaluate a script or a performance. It makes Oscars.

But there are other aspects of this scene that are important to a writer. What is this tableau? What is its metaphor? Who are we? Where are we? Who are the guys we're concerned with?

"We're in a lounge . . ."

And what is this lounge?

Somebody gets a brilliant notion. "It's a theater!"

Bravo! It's a theater and we are the audience and the two guys are the actors. Now these actors are manipulating the audience at will, taking them up and down the ladder of emotion. Just as it should be in a successful play or movie. The audience has completely forgotten itself and is wholly concentrated on the conflict.

Now I'm going to throw you a curve. What if the two combatants are really actors? Putting the audience on? Would the audience react differently in that case?

"Does the audience know they're actors?"

No.

"Then it would be the same."

If! If! If *what*?

The students looked perplexed.

If they were *believable*! If the audience guessed they were actors, playing a joke, there would be no emotional response, except, perhaps amusement. But this is a template for what we're trying to do. What everyone in show business is trying to do.

Next time we will have the most important session in the course. We're going to learn what a story is.

ASSIGNMENT: A SINGLES BAR. A GUY IS TRYING TO PICK UP A GIRL. THREE OR FOUR PAGES. ENOUGH COPIES FOR ALL CHARACTERS.

CLASS TWO
THE STORY

In 15 minutes he explained to me what a story is and how to come up with a story and how to know if you have a story.
—Rob Lotterstein,
Creator/Executive Producer,
The War at Home

Results of the Class One assignment. (I am not going to present the actual scripts from the students because I'm afraid it would be a lot of not very interesting reading material.)

At this moment they are a bit nervous and reluctant. No one wants to go first. But finally a girl brings out her copies, casts people from around the table to read, and we're off. After the scene is read, I ask for comments.

Nobody speaks—this is par for the course. And I don't have a lot to say either. This is the first attempt, and nobody knows anything yet. But I feel obligated to point out some fundamental things that will be helpful in the future.

First, there are way too many stage directions. This always happens in early assignments. People try to tell the story in the stage directions. They offer too much information about the characters they are introducing, including what they're all about and even what's on their mind. I point out that the audience cannot read the stage directions and must learn about the characters from what they do and say. Even in submitting material, it's a bad idea to have stage directions that are too detailed. The reader doesn't want to get his information from the stage directions. He is much happier to deduce what the character is like from his actions and dialogue.

For another thing, actors hate to have the writer indicate what their attitude is. Directions, such as: amused, irritated, frowning, smiling, etc. make the actors want to spit. After all, they are actors. They know what to do.

Another thing: One of the characters falls into the *bar trap*. This is where an actor takes a page or more to order a drink. The drink he wants is very complicated, of course, but so what? What does it prove? The audience wants to see the encounter begin. This only serves the cowardly writer who wants to delay a bit before tackling the nitty-gritty.

◆ ❖ ◆

When I tell students that hardly anybody knows what a story is, not even professional writers in Hollywood, they look at me as if I'm daft. How could people who make a living telling stories not know what a story is? Well, in my experience, most professional writers tell stories by the seat of their pants. They know what it feels like to have a story when they're writing. And they know what it feels like when they have no story or a weak story. But most of them couldn't explain what a story *is* if their lives depended on it. Oh, they'll give explanations of what a story is, but it won't help anybody *write* a story, and few of them use their own definition when they write.

The first five years of my writing career in TV were in the freelance mode. That meant you went in to see a producer with a bunch of notions and you hammered out a story with the one that he liked the best. It might take a day, two days, a week, but you stuck with it and you wound up with enough for a first draft. Then you (with a partner or without) went home and fleshed it out. Then you turned it in. A few days later you had a call to come in for notes. The producer told you what he wanted changed, and you did it. When you turned in this second draft, you were through. You got a check and any other changes were done without you.

During these years I knew practically all my fellow comedy writers. I saw them at lunch and around town and at interviews and I assumed they were competent professionals who were well versed in their trade. Then my partner, Harvey Miller, and I got an office job as story editors on a new show—*Love, American Style*.

We weren't aware that most of the best writers in the business had rejected the job. It was an anthology, an hour show that had four or five stories in it. Most writers had all they could do to produce one story a week, and here they were asking for three or four! We stewed over how that could be done. At last we settled on a strategy. We would call every agent in town and tell them we wanted to see every freelance writer they had, and we would set up appointments. We really needed stories, and quick. We saw three writers or teams in the morning, had lunch, and saw three more in the afternoon.

Well, I was shocked. Hardly any of the writers who came in to sell us stories, had any real idea of what a story was! They said stuff like, "A really funny thing happened when my wife and I were dating . . . I'm not sure it's a story, but it was really funny." Or, "There was an incident . . . whether it's a story or not you'll have to judge."

What usually happened was that if Harvey and I thought there was any promise in the morsel that was offered, we jumped in and pitched with the writer, exploring any possibility that a story would emerge, and often it did, but it was gut-wrenching work. And this is where I first used the tape recorder. I figured that without the little machine our recollection of the day's work would be nothing but a blur. And it had another unexpected advantage. When writers came in with their first draft and we found that it in no way resembled the story that we'd pitched, we threw it in the waste basket and did the story ourselves, using the tape.

After the first season, Doug Cramer, the head of TV at Paramount, had us come into his office. He said, "Well, the show has mediocre ratings and we're losing eighteen thousand a month on it. Furthermore, ABC is lukewarm about it. I know it's a son-of-a-bitch to produce. No one thought it could be done. You guys have done a remarkable job putting it on the air.

"As I see it, we've got two choices and I want your input about what we should do. We can declare victory and go home feeling good about it. Or we can try to keep it going. What's your answer?"

It took us only a moment. "We want to keep it going!" Cramer looked surprised. But he shrugged and said, "O.K."

ABC cut the show to a half-hour and made Harvey and me the producers. Billy De Angelo, the erstwhile producer, went on to produce *Barefoot in the Park*, a pilot that Harvey and I had written based on the Neil Simon play.

We were fired after that second season. But the show went on for another five years, leaving me with two strong convictions. One was that our work on the show those first two seasons had given impetus to its continued life, and two, that our knowledge of story had made it work. The proof that our competence was not in question was the fact that after we were fired we were immediately rehired by Paramount as story editors of *The Odd Couple*, a top-ten show.

So I ask the class: What is a story?

"It has a beginning, a middle and an end."

Always the first answer. And I tell them what Mel Brooks said when they told him that. "So has a piece of shit."

There were other answers. None that would help them write a story. They fumble around some more, repeating all the misinformation they'd learned in school. Finally they are tired and frustrated and I offer to tell them what a story is.

"Yeah! Tell us!"

O.K. You need three elements to tell a story. What are they?

"Protagonist."

Let's call him the hero.

"Why?"

Because he is a hero. Our hero. And it's easier. But remember—the hero does not need to be heroic. He can be a crook, a shyster, a con-man, a mobster, anything, just so long as he wants something and the audience empathizes with him.

"O.K."

What do you need next?

"Villain."

Not next. Something else comes first.

"Something the hero wants?"

Right. His goal.

"*Next* is villain."

Let's call him the obstacle. Now those three elements can be diagrammed. Bill goes to the board. Here's what he draws:

This is the anatomy of every story ever told. Can you believe that? Let's test it out. *Moby Dick*. Who's the hero?

"Ahab."

Right. What's his goal?

"Kill the whale."

Right. What's the obstacle?

"The whale."

Right. That's the way it is in many stories; the goal and the obstacle are the same. James Bond in *Dr. No*. Who's the hero?

"Bond."

What's his goal?

"Get Dr.No."

What's the obstacle?

"Dr. No."

Let's get classical. *Romeo and Juliet*. Who's the hero?

"Romeo."

What's his goal?

"Juliet."

What's the obstacle?

"The family."

O.K. Now you suggest a play or movie.

"*My Fair Lady*."

Good. Who's the hero?

"Eliza Doolittle."

No. Who has the goal?

"Professor Higgins."

Right, he's the one we're going to root for. He has the problem and the story is about whether he will succeed or not. So he's the hero. Get it?

(Dubious) "Well, yeah . . ."

It'll become clearer. What's his goal?

"To make Eliza into a lady."

Right. What's the obstacle?

"Eliza."

Correctamunday. See how it works?

(Nods)

There are four kinds of stories. Here they are:

1) Man vs. man. Ninety percent of stories are this kind.

2) Man vs. animals. Maybe five percent.

3) Man vs. the elements. Three percent.

4) Man vs. himself. Two percent. Let's have another story. Maybe Man vs. himself.

"*Leaving Las Vegas.*"

Excellent. Who's the hero?

"Nicolas Cage."

Right. What's his goal?

"To commit suicide."

On the button. What's the obstacle?

"His girlfriend. The prostitute."

Right! By George, I think you've got it! I'll pitch you a curve. Everybody see *Moonstruck*?

"Yeah."

O.K. Who's the hero?

"Cher."

Right. What does she want?

"To get married."

Oh-oh. Not so fast! It's not that simple. What sort of marriage is she looking for?

"A happy marriage."

Not necessarily. Don't forget she's been brainwashed by her mother.

(Blank stares)

Don't you remember what her mother tells her, over and over? No? "When love enters the picture, you got trouble."

"Oh, yeah . . ."

So what sort of marriage is she looking for? A loveless marriage. And in the first scene she's getting it. A big schlub is on his knees in an Italian restaurant and he's hired violins . . .

"Yeah, yeah . . ."

Then he leaves to see his sick mother in Italy and she meets his brother, Nicolas Cage, who has only one hand . . . and he comes on to her but she's scared to death of him. Why? What does he represent?

"Love!"

Exactly. Who would figure out a story like that—where love is the obstacle? An ingenious writer, that's who. That's why the picture was so intriguing. And made so much money. Well, that's enough for today. Next time we'll look into some other aspects of the story.

ASSIGNMENT: REDO THE PREVIOUS ASSIGNMENT WITH WISDOM GLEANED FROM THIS CLASS ON STORY.

CLASS THREE
RAMIFICATIONS OF THE STORY

A lot of times you read a bad script and the first couple of pages are just jokes because people think, "If I'm clever enough, that's all that's going to matter," but with Idelson, you really had to get to the story point blank, right away . . . what's going on, why should you care about these characters?
—Aron Abrams,
Co-Executive Producer,
King of the Hill

Results of assignment: They were somewhat better, and some students thought they were a lot better, until I began pointing out a few things.

What does the guy want?

"To make an impression on the girl."

He wants to get laid, right? He's the hero. And what does *she* want?

"*Not* to get laid."

Not by him, anyway. She's the obstacle. Why does she talk to him?

"She tells him she's not interested."

Right. But she continues the conversation. She's sending a mixed message. As long as she keeps talking, we feel he's got a chance. To be a proper obstacle she's got to make us believe there's no chance. But he keeps trying because he really wants to get laid. The irresistible force meets the immovable object. We have a struggle, which is what will keep the audience interested, right?

"Right. But what should she do? Refuse to talk?"

Why not? In real life, would that be so strange? Lots of girls have refused to talk to me in bars. She might even call the bartender over and tell him the guy is bothering her, and the bartender says he'd better quit or get thrown out. The more impossible you make it for the hero, the better. But the guy is horny, extremely horny, and he has to think up ways to get the girl's attention. Now doesn't that intrigue you more? Don't hold back. Go all out. That way the money lurks.

Note: I won't critique every scene done by the students, but select one, or maybe two, that represent a general fault.

◆ ❖ ◆

When you first saw the diagram I drew of the story, I'm sure you thought it looked kind of childish. And I told you it represented every story ever told. If I'm telling the truth, how come? How can that little insignificant sketch be so important, so meaningful?

They murmured things. Someone said, "It's life."

I pointed at him. Exactly! Exactly! It's the way life works! When you wake up in the morning, this is you (pointing at the hero). It's Everyman. You want something: a girl, a guy, a job, a raise and there's an obstacle: the girl, the guy, the boss. The story is the *struggle* to get what you want, what the *hero* wants. The story is the *struggle*; the more difficult the struggle, the stronger the story.

How do you make it more difficult? Well, it's the irresistible force against the immovable object. The hero has got to desire the goal a *lot*. The obstacle has got to be unyielding. The audience has got to believe there is no solution. If you can make them believe that, they'll be on the edge of their seats. The hero cannot give up. The obstacle cannot give up. The longer the impasse the longer the audience will pay attention. The minute one side surrenders, the story is over. The story is the *struggle*.

James Bond faces extraordinary obstacles, larger than life. And James goes through hell before he wins out. As a matter of fact, the audience can't see how he will emerge from some of the fixes the obstacle puts him in. Of course! They're spending millions and millions of dollars. The struggle has to be enormous!

But you say, "I just want to write a simple little sitcom that'll make people laugh. What has all this stupendous drama of James

Bond got to do with me?" Well, baby, the principle is the same. The hero of your sitcom has to face an obstacle that is as difficult for him as Dr. No is to James Bond. It might be that his kid wants to join a gang. He's worried that his wife is playing around. The obstacle is as large in *his* world as the enemy is in Bond's.

The term "sitcom" is short for situation comedy. That means a situation is created that will lead to a struggle in a comedy vein. But it has more significance than that. Every story is a *situation* story. We can call other sorts of stories "situation-horror" stories, "situation-suspense" stories, "situation-sex," "situation-action," "situation-tragic," "situation-melodrama," "situation-satire," etc. You get the picture. The writer creates a situation that produces strong emotion in the audience. We, as writers, must understand that making the juices flow is our main objective and any manner of story that accomplishes that is legitimate. Of course, the emotion desired must follow the tenor of the story all the way through. In other words, it is not advised to write a story that begins as a comedy and turns into tragedy. Or vice versa.

So when does a story start? You've probably had the experience of someone touting a book, but says something like this: "You've got to have patience with this book. It takes a while to get interesting. But once it gets going you won't be able to put it down." This means the story starts late. It's sort of dangerous for the writer, and tedious for the reader. It is much more important to start the story quickly, on the first few lines if possible, certainly in the first few pages. So how does a story start quickly? When does a story start?

The students mull this over.

"When the hero is introduced."

No.

"When you know what the hero wants."

Uh-uh.

"We give up."

When all three of the ingredients are established: The hero, goal and obstacle. When all three of those are known, the story starts.

"How do you do that?"

Well, we had that problem in *Love, American Style*. The show had several stories, and when one ended and the next one hadn't start-ed, it was a dangerous time. That's when the audience went to the kitchen for a soda or to the bathroom for a pee, or used the remote to change channels. We were well aware of those dangers and constructed our stories to avoid them.

I remember one, off the top of my head, to illustrate how we did it. The scene is an elegant dining room. A young man in his twenties is seated at one end of a long table. His mother, a dowager, is seated at the other end. A butler is at the sideboard, preparing to serve breakfast.

The young man speaks. "Mother, there's someone I'd like to bring here this evening. A young woman I . . . I'd like you to meet."

"Where'd you find this one, Jack?" answers the mother.

Has the story started? Who's the hero? Jack. What's his goal? To present a girl to his mother whom he hopes will earn his mother's approval. What's the obstacle? The mother. Hero, goal and obstacle are all established in two lines of dialogue. The audience is piqued enough to give us a little more time to set the hook. And that's the way it's done.

ASSIGNMENT: TWO PSYCHIATRISTS. THE YOUNGER ONE IS HAVING AN AFFAIR WITH THE OLDER ONE'S WIFE. THE WIFE INSISTS THAT HER LOVER GO TO HER HUSBAND AND TELL HIM THEIR SECRET. RELUCTANTLY, THE LOVER MAKES AN APPOINTMENT AND GOES TO SEE THE BETRAYED HUSBAND IN HIS OFFICE. WE BEGIN WRITING WHEN THE YOUNG LOVER ENTERS THE OTHER MAN'S OFFICE.

CLASS FOUR
MORE RAMIFICATIONS

Somebody told me in advance that he sets you up to fail in those exercises so you can start from the ground up. You realize, "I do have a lot to learn. I'm not the big shot I thought I was."
—Sherry Bilsing,
Co-Executive Producer,
Friends

Results of assignment: The students are generally pleased with each other's work, and their own, I might add. However, the mean instructor roots out flaws as usual.

Why does the lover blurt out that he is fucking the older man's wife as soon as he comes into the office?

"I thought you said to start the story as soon as possible."

I did. But is it realistic? Besides, the story starts when he comes into the office. Would things really happen the way you wrote it?

"Maybe not."

Absolutely not. The lover would introduce himself. *Establish* himself. Maybe even be flattering about the older man's reputation. The younger man has read the other guy's books. The lover wants this encounter to go as painlessly as possible. Wouldn't *you*?

Maybe the lover modestly gives some of his own résumé to establish that he is a man of substance. Perhaps he uses some of his skills as a therapist to soften the older man up.

Now what does the older man do? He is the obstacle. He is obliged to make the interview go as roughly as possible. He makes a scene, an ugly one. Get it? O.K.

But the reason we must not omit the obligatory polite routine of two men in the same business, meeting for the first time, is that the reality of that situation sets the reality of the whole scene for the audience. If they abrogate the formalities of their meeting, the audience is going to have a hard time believing any of it.

◆　❖　◆

Why do we need a hero? Well, because we're paying ten dollars, or nearly ten dollars to see the movie.

What sort of smart-ass statement is that? It's true, that's the joke. The hero is the guy we're rooting for, and as the story unfolds, we empathize with him. If the story is done skillfully, we take another giant step: We *become* the hero. This means we experience all that the hero does. We accept the blows as well as the triumphs. For two hours or so we live the life of the hero and share his adventure.

Did you think people pay ten dollars just to hear some clever dialogue or ogle some gorgeous girls? No, hell no! We want to live a different life than the one we spend in our dull day-to-day existence. For two hours we want to live the life of a cowboy, a gunslinger, a fighter pilot, James Bond. We want to shoot the buttons off a villain's vest, ride a spaceship, make love to Miss America. The hero is the guy every man in the audience wants to be and the one the women want to love.

Why does the bullfight persist in our culture? Why does the boxer draw our cheers? The wrestler, even though it's phony as hell? The acrobat, the pilot at the air show, the driver at Indy? Because when we view the event, we're fighting the champ, the bully, the bull. We're flying the plane and driving the race car.

Mainly we're living a different life. One of danger, adventure, love, pain, victory. And this is all through the magic of the story. Incidentally, the hero can be a multiple entity: The Three Musketeers, The Marx Brothers, The Dodgers, The Lakers, The Rams. Likewise, the obstacle can be multiple: The Nazis, the King's Men, the Police.

Why do we need a goal? Because it gives reason to the story. And gives us a feeling, probably false, that there's a meaning to life. It gives us momentum. It gives us purpose.

Why do we have an obstacle? Because without one there's no struggle, and the story is the struggle. The more formidable the obstacle, the more riveting the story.

One thing we haven't talked about yet. What are those little dashes under the story diagram?

"Steps," says a girl.

Right. Steps to what?

"The hero's goal."

Right. And what do we call those steps?

Blank looks.

Scenes. Stories are told in scenes. At least in movies, plays and TV. What are they called in novels?

"Chapters."

Correct. And they are very important. As I say, stories are told in scenes. The scenes are steps toward the hero's goal. Opposed by the obstacle. You wouldn't believe how confused beginning writers can be about scenes. They'll say something like, "Boy, have I got a great scene! The hero and his girlfriend are up in a Ferris wheel. And down below, the bad guys are running around looking for them . . ."

Wait a minute! They're on a desert island . . .

"Yeah, but . . ."

The scenes have got to follow the story! The audience must follow what is happening. It's a great scene, but it doesn't fit the story!

"I guess you're right."

(This is an exaggeration. None of my students have ever proposed anything this ridiculous. But I'm trying to make a point with overkill. Each scene must be in a natural sequence to one that has gone before. We're taking the audience on a journey and it must be a series of steps that evolve logically.)

Back to starting the story. Can you imagine a movie that begins before a word is spoken? Did you see *Butch Cassidy and the Sundance Kid*? Well, that brilliant film began just that way.

Butch (Paul Newman) enters a bank and looks around. There is a series of shots from his POV. A look at the people in line to get to the teller. The teller counting out money. A shot of the guard standing by, pan down to his gun. A shot of the open vault, showing the safe. It is a gleaming steel affair with doors several inches thick, and looks impenetrable.

Butch walks over to the guard and says: "What happened to the *old* bank that was here?"

"People kept robbin' it," says the guard.

Butch looks at him querulously. "A small price to pay for beauty," he says, and walks out.

Has the story started? Before anyone speaks? Who's the hero? Butch. What does he want? To rob the bank. What's the obstacle? The formidable safe, a symbol of the new, modern world that will eventually claim the lives of Butch and Sundance. And all three elements are established before a line of dialogue.

ASSIGNMENT: TWO COLLEGE PROFESSORS. THE GUY IS A PROFESSOR OF ARCHEOLOGY, THE WIFE TEACHES ANTHROPOLOGY. THEY LOVE EACH OTHER. THEY HAVE AN ACTIVE SEX LIFE. FOR THE LAST SIX MONTHS SHE HAS BEEN IN AFRICA, COMMUNICATING WITH GORILLAS, AND HE HAS NEARLY GONE CRAZY WITH LONELINESS AND HORNINESS. NOW SHE ARRIVES HOME AND HE IS DELIRIOUS TO SEE HER, HE WANTS TO HEAR ABOUT HER TRIP, BUT HE IS ALSO ANXIOUS TO GET HER INTO BED. SHE SAYS, "HOLD ON, I HAVE A SURPRISE FOR YOU," AND GOES TO THE DOOR TO ADMIT A GORILLA. YOU BEGIN WRITING WHEN THE WIFE ARRIVES HOME.

CLASS FIVE
DIALOGUE

We all shy away from conflict and everyone makes the same mistakes class after class, assignment after assignment, year after year. The gorilla sketch . . . everyone has to do it three or four times because nobody wants to write conflict.
—Ellen Idelson,
Co-Creator/Executive Producer,
Sixteen to Life

Results of assignment: People have had a good time with this exercise, but have made some significant mistakes.

Why did you make the gorilla a female?

"I don't know. Why not?"

Well, the husband's the hero and he wants his wife back, for a lot of reasons. He's been lonely without her, he's missed sex with her, the whole package. That's the goal. What's the obstacle?

"The gorilla."

Right! So what's the more formidable obstacle, a virile, young male gorilla with balls like a pawnshop, or a nice, passive female?

"You didn't say it had to be a male."

I didn't say *anything* about the gorilla. Intentionally. I wanted you to work it out for yourself. But which gender would make the stronger obstacle? Especially if there seemed to be an emotional attachment between the wife and the gorilla?

Laughter and protests. "Hey! You didn't say that, either!"

You're right. But I'm trying to get you to make the story as strong as possible. To think like a professional. *Intensify* the struggle. I believe a professional writer would automatically take that path. What *is* this situation that we're presenting here?

Blank looks.

A triangle! Like a Noel Coward play! Two men and a woman. Even though one of the men is a gorilla! What would be the greatest threat to the husband's goal of resuming the perfect union with his wife? A gorilla (man) who loves his wife!

They saw the wisdom of this choice, reluctantly.

You didn't want to go this route because it was too difficult. But that's the name of the game. Listen, you're walking down a dark street at night. Coming toward you is a really menacing-looking guy. What do you do?

Pause. "Cross over to the other side of the street."

Sure. That's a normal human reaction. But the writer mustn't do that. He's got to walk right up to the guy, and say something like, "What's your problem, bub?" That's what makes the juices flow. The writer must not avoid conflict.

They nod. Bill points at a girl. You made the gorilla a *baby* gorilla.

"Yeah . . ."

For the same reason. You avoided the conflict. I call it "diminishing the obstacle." During my years of teaching writing, I've seen all kinds of ways of avoiding conflict with the gorilla. Female gorillas, baby gorillas, apes, orangutans, sedated gorillas, caged gorillas, caged sedated gorillas, spider monkeys . . .

They're laughing now.

There's no limit to the lengths a beginning writer will go to avoid conflict. The easy way out. Don't do it. *Intensify* the conflict if you want to make a living.

We had a story for *Love, American Style* that involved an African-American couple. The husband comes home to find his wife in a state. It seems that coming up in the elevator this afternoon, the only other passenger in the elevator, a black male, had pinched her ass. The husband is furious. He intends to beat the other man to a pulp. Fortunately, his wife knows where this scoundrel lives: Apt. 624.

He rushes up there, hammers on the door. The man who opens it is six-three, about two hundred and twenty pounds wearing a T-shirt that exposes arms like tree trunks. Our hero is a little guy, about five-six, and realizes he's in trouble. He stutters something and the big guy asks gently if his visitor wants an autograph.

"Autograph?"

"Yeah. You know who I am, don't you?"

"No . . ."

"Mike Boss, 'The Bone Crusher.' I'm wrestling for the World Championship next Wednesday."

"Oh . . ."

"I thought maybe you wanted an autograph . . ."

"Uh, no, I got the wrong apartment . . ."

"Oh. O.K." Mike nods and closes the door. Our husband goes back downstairs and tells his wife he gave the miscreant a good talking-to and set him straight. There are more developments to the story but they're not pertinent here.

We heard that Sonny Liston, who had just fought Mohammed Ali for the World's Boxing Championship, was available and he was good for the fighter, but we wanted Sammy Davis, Jr. for the husband and the rumor was that he didn't like Sonny. Somebody had to go up and see Sammy, and talk him into doing the show, but no one wanted to go, because Sammy Davis was known as kind of a nasty guy. I said blithely that I would go. What could he do to me?

Sammy lived in Bel Air. Way up in Bel Air, at the top of a hill, and the house was a castle. I parked and walked up a million stairs to the front door. I rang the bell and waited. And waited. I rang the bell again. And waited some more. What the hell, Paramount had called him and told him I was coming. It didn't occur to me that no one appeared at the door because he *knew* I was coming. Anyway, finally the door opened a crack and a maid peered out at me. I told her I was there to see Mr. Davis. The door closed and I waited again. I was getting pissed off, but I was determined to wait them out.

Eventually the door opened again and the maid, without a word, ushered me into a sitting room where two guys who looked like bodyguards were standing. One said, "Mr. Davis is on the phone. Sit down." I sat. The goons sat, too. One of them picked up a newspaper, the other lit a cigarette.

We cooled our heels like that for almost an hour. I asked the men how long they expected Sammy to be busy. "It's long distance," said one.

Maybe it wasn't quite two hours, but it seemed like it. One of the men said, "You can go up now. Upstairs, first door on the right."

I went up and into Sammy's bedroom. The little star was sitting at a table, smoking a cigarette in a long silver holder. He indicated the chair across from him without looking at me.

"What's the piece about?" he asked.

I told him, briefly.

"Why do you want Liston?"

"Well, we think he's right for the part."

"What's the matter with Ali?"

I shook my head. There was no sense in explaining that Liston was a better obstacle. "No, the guy has got to look tough. Like an animal."

"Ali could tear you apart."

"Sure, but he looks like a nice guy, with a sense of humor. He looks like you could reason with him."

"I don't like Liston. Have you hired him already?"

I nodded.

"Well, send me a script. I'll let you know."

"O.K. Thanks very much."

We never heard from Sammy and took that as a refusal. We hired Godfrey Cambridge to do Sammy's part. But the difficulties with Sonny were not over. He came into town and went directly to the studios.

I was off somewhere, and my partner, Harvey Miller, was alone in our office. Harvey was a Woody Allen type, a neurotic New York Jew, very nervous. He told me about his encounter with Sonny Liston. The giant fighter came directly to the desk.

"Who're you?" asked Sonny.

"Harvey Miller. You're Sonny Liston, right?"

"Yeah. Where do you live?"

"In the Valley . . ."

"House or apartment?"

"Uh . . . I got a house . . ."

"Uh-huh. I'm gonna move in with you . . ."

"What?"

"I'm movin' in for the week I'm doin' the show. I can't go to a motel, understand?"

"No, but . . ."

"I won't bother you. But you're not expectin' any company, are ya?"

"Well, no . . ."

"Good. I don't want no other people . . ."

"Oh . . ."

"Write down the address."

Harvey was too frightened to do anything else. He wrote the address and Liston took it and left. He stayed with Harvey for the week he did the show, and Harvey was a nervous wreck during the time the fighter was there.

A couple of years later we heard that Sonny had checked into a hotel in Vegas and was found dead in his room the next morning, apparently from an overdose.

But the real moral of the story is that in order to make our episode work, we had to have an obstacle, a *real* obstacle. Even though Mohammed Ali was a tougher guy than Sonny Liston, and proved it by knocking Sonny out later, when they fought, his personality was inferior as an obstacle for our story. Ali was a cheerful sort. Our husband, the hero, probably could have prevailed on Ali's good nature and got his sympathy for the husband's dilemma.

Every person wants something every moment of his life, from the instant he's born to the minute he dies.

You want something right now. You want to understand what I'm saying, or perhaps you're looking to catch me in a discrepancy, so you can claim I'm full of shit. I want to get an idea across to you. A baby wants to eat, or sleep, or cry. He wants the person approaching him to smile or maybe refrain from throwing him in the air, as it appears he intends to do.

I hope you believe me. If not, test it. Catch yourself at any moment and see if you want anything. It doesn't have to be a profound thing. Maybe you just want to be left alone. There was an intriguing film made on that premise. Charles Laughton in *The Beachcomber*. All he wanted was to be left alone, and as you probably surmise, all hell breaks loose.

But if everybody wants something at all times, what is it they want?

"Happiness?"

Yeah . . .

"Love?"

Sure . . .

"Contentment?"

Listen, everything you're saying is true. But I want a generic answer, an umbrella that covers it all.

Blank looks.

O.K. I'll tell you. Everybody wants what is in *their* own best interest. And this means *everybody at all times*. Even Mother Theresa. Get it? Believe it?

"Yeah . . ."

Now if we accept the principle that we all want what is in our own best interest, it becomes a really important bit of knowledge in our writing. If everyone wants what is in his own best interest, what happens when people get together? A clash of interests. Conflict!

How often do two people want the exact same thing—at the exact same time? It used to be difficult for me to write a scene where there were a lot of people, like a party, for instance. But once I ascribed specific *wants* to the various individuals, it became a lot easier, more fun, and also more realistic, because that's what happens in life.

Suppose two girls get an apartment together. They're roommates. How often would you guess that one wants the place to be warmer when the other wants it cooler? When one wants the blinds up and the other wants them down? How about marriage? How many discussions end in arguments? How many divorces occur for the simple reason the two partners can never seem to agree?

Think of Congress. How many bills pass without wrangling and amendments? Think of the two political parties. Do they ever see things the same? Think of people in a lifeboat. In a jail cell. In a public meeting. On a first date. Conflict! Much more often than not.

But back to wants, and don't forget they're present every second throughout our lives. There are only two ways to get what we want. Your Final Draft® software indicates what they are. Two settings: Action and Dialogue. In primitive places and times, such as the old west, action was the key, or at least that's what we're led to believe. But in our civilization, dialogue is used more. There is no more fascinating and complex a subject than dialogue. It's a subject for a lifetime study, and it better be a long life.

Do people say what they want? Well, it varies—a *lot*. It depends on so many things. Their age, their character, the situation, what's at stake, etc. Do they ever say the *opposite* of what they want? Damn right! Because it suits their interest. So how do we ever get a handle on realistic dialogue?

Well, it's the same as in acting. We must put ourselves in the mind and body of our character, take on the conditions mentioned above, and play with the possibilities. At this point let me put in another word for the tape recorder. I am a great fan of the tape recorder. In my book, it's the most valuable tool in the writer's arsenal. Improvise with it. Tape is cheap, and no one needs to know what foolish things you might have tried. When you play it back, you'll get a good idea of what sounds real and what doesn't. Get to be friends with the tape recorder. It will pay enormous dividends, though it may take a while to get comfortable with it.

O.K. How do we know we're writing realistically, being faithful to the characters and the situation? Well, one thing is in our favor. Most of us, instinctively, are pretty good judges of human nature and behavior. After all, we've lived around other people all our lives, we can anticipate what they might do or say. But we can also improve in that regard, by being observant of other people, in intimate situations and in groups. Write down conversation, even bits of conversation you've heard. Again, the tape recorder is an invaluable asset. And don't hesitate to use it surreptitiously. Most people don't mind, even if they catch you, and it's worth the risk. An improvisation class can be helpful. Acting classes likewise.

Writing is rewriting. Ever hear that?

Nods.

What do we do when we rewrite? We intensify: The situation, the conflict, the struggle. When the struggle becomes unbearable, we're on the right track!

O.K. Let's sum it up. What's the difference between good dialogue and bad dialogue? What's the difference between dialogue that leaps off the page and makes people claw into their wallets to get into the theatre, cluster around the TV to watch a show they never miss, or "chuffa-chuffa" (the writer's name for meaningless chit-chat) as turned out by the denizens of the Hollywood Hills?

Well, bad dialogue is engendered by the writer, and motivated by his desires, which are to write clever conversation, jokes, and show how smart he is and how much he knows, like the builder of a bad refrigerator. He wants to inflate his ego and speak to the audience, something the audience is bored by and won't pay for. Good dialogue is spoken by the character, generally to another character, and makes the audience believe what they are watching is really happening. It makes audiences' juices flow and holds their attention and puts money in the writer's pocket.

How does the writer achieve this desirable end? Well, this is where the artistry comes in. The writer must become an actor and get into the body, soul, and mind of the character. He must *become* the character, motivated by the desires of that individual, and behave accordingly. A good acting class can be valuable, an improvisation class likewise, and psychotherapy is probably the best preparation there is. Most good writers usually log a lot of hours on the couch.

ASSIGNMENT: REDO PREVIOUS ASSIGNMENT.

CLASS SIX
DIALOGUE AND CHARACTER

For weeks Bill kept telling me, "Take a tape recorder and record people talking." Finally I took his advice and a whole new world opened up to me: the way people really talk.
—Steve Atinsky,
Author,
Tyler on Prime Time

A child wants something different than an older person, isn't that true? A boy wants something different than a girl. A boy from the wrong side of the tracks wants something different than a boy from an upper-class neighborhood, no? We can expand this to all the differences between people of different age, different gender, different circumstances, including childhood environment. All those factors register on what a certain individual wants and *how he tries to get it*. That's the other half of the equation. What he wants is particular to his age, his situation and his upbringing, and so is the way he tries to *get* what he wants.

You can see that what a person is, with all the different factors that influence his personality, determines the person he shows himself to be. But the essence is *expressed* by what he wants and how he goes about getting it. So that's the way we should think about character. What does he want and how does he try to get it?

Casting is important. Your story can be more or less effective, depending on the characters. If Captain Ahab had the personality of a bank clerk, Moby Dick would not exist. The character is key to the emotion we want to evoke. A clean-cut all-American boy might not be as useful in a horror picture as a slimy guy. A passive girl would probably not work as well in a romantic comedy as a capricious one.

ASSIGNMENT: WE HAVE AN ATTRACTIVE GIRL. SHE IS A MACHO GIRL, THE KIND WE USED TO CALL A "TOMBOY." HER HOBBY IS SKYDIVING, AND SHE DOES IT EVERY WEEKEND. HER DREAM IS TO GET MARRIED IN A FREE-FALL FROM 15,000 FEET, AND THOUGH SHE'S HAD MANY SUITORS THEY'VE ALL BEEN REJECTED BECAUSE THEY WERE TOO CHICKEN TO GET MARRIED IN THAT MANNER. BUT FINALLY SHE'S FOUND A GUY THAT'S UP TO SNUFF. HE'S WILLING TO DO THE FREE-FALL EVEN THOUGH HE'S NEVER DONE IT BEFORE. HE LOVES THIS GIRL MORE THAN LIFE ITSELF. THEY ARE IN THE PLANE, READY FOR THE JUMP, THREE MINUTES FROM THE DROP, AND WE BEGIN WRITING.

CLASS SEVEN
THE SCAM

*Growing up in my house, my dad would hide a tape recorder
somewhere in the kitchen during dinner. I guess that was his
way of capturing realistic family dinner conversation.
Invariably at some point one of us four kids would spot the
hidden tape recorder and get really pissed off and whine,
"Dad . . . not the tape recorder again!"*
**—Ellen Idelson,
Co-Creator/Executive Producer,
*Sixteen to Life***

Results of the assignment. Everybody does the same thing. He
chickens out and admits he's scared. She loves him anyway, or
maybe she doesn't.

Bill says they are taking the easy road, and writers mustn't do that
if they want to earn a living at it. What the hero wants above all is
the girl, and he knows she's rejected all the other suitors for lack of
guts. He decides the only solution is to bluff it through, pretending
to be having the time of his life even though he's incoherent with
fear. The struggle is with himself. This is a much tougher road to hoe,
but it leads to a funnier, more interesting scene, do you see that?

◆ ❖ ◆

All good writers conduct a scam. So do actors, directors, producers,
scenic designers and costumers.

Can you guess what it is?

Blank looks. It seemed like even the *idea* of scamming was
foreign to these students' concept of good writing.

Well, I'll tell you. And it's a trick you appreciate when you're part
of the audience. It's the idea that you are watching something that
is happening *at this very moment, at this time and place*. You're
looking at a real bedroom, a park, or a subway platform. These are

the actual characters in the story. And what is happening on the stage or on the screen is actually going on at this very instant. If the scam works, you are in for a great experience. Your juices will flow and you will live the life that is being portrayed on stage. It may not occur at every moment in the performance, but even if it only happens sporadically it is worth every penny for the ticket.

In a flop show you will be aware of being seated in a theater seat. There are actors on stage that are obviously saying things they memorized from a script written by a writer. Somebody is coughing. A kid is complaining. You are spending a tedious evening. Your feet hurt.

So how do you write to make the audience forget completely about sitting in a theater seat and bring them into the scene? Huh?

"Make it real."

Sure. How?

"I don't know . . ."

Well, you've got to imitate life. You've got to make it seem that your characters are not on a stage, but in real surroundings, responding to an actual situation, to people who are as real as they are. And remember this: People are full of thoughts, memories and feelings at all times. They react to what is said and done by other people according to those thoughts, memories and feelings, sometimes violently.

The students look distressed. This is hard. It's going to require a lot of work.

It's not as hard as it seems. You've got to analyze the difference between acting on a stage and living a life. And pretend that you're doing the latter. Actors on stage are saying and doing things set out for them by a writer and director. So you've got to make the audience believe there is no writer or director. Writer and director must take a hike. The writer certainly must fade away. Now, this may explain why the writers in the Hollywood Hills make no money. The last thing they want to do is disappear!

But people in life do not have a writer feeding them lines as they go about living. So the audience must believe that the actors are behaving according to their own desires. The things they say and the things they do must seem to be what *they want* to do. Or have to do. And good actors certainly aid in this deception. One thing that can help is to be aware of what happens in dialogue, for instance. One character speaks. The words enter the other character's ears. They go to the brain where they register. The receiving person must evaluate. The filters in his brain check through and examine possible hidden meanings. Is she putting him on? Or is she coming on to him? Then he must choose an answer. One seems too flippant. Another seems too weak. One seems too aggressive. Another seems to send the wrong message. Finally, an acceptable reply presents itself, and is expressed.

Whoa! That will take ages. The characters on stage will stand and look silently at each other for a long pause every time the other one speaks. Not at all. The whole process takes a nanosecond. The human brain is the fastest computer known. It makes all other computers look sluggish. The process is in effect during the most rapid *bang-bang* repartee. But the writer and the actor must be *aware* of the dynamics to make it seem real. The writer must let the scene *breathe*.

If all this seems mystical, I can only say it's what happens in real life and must be observed to operate the scam.

The deportment of the actors must also be motivated by their character's personality and background. Rocky will not respond like Inspector Clouseau. All this, at this time, must seem terribly complex, and it is. But this is the road you've chosen and it's a long one.

What will keep you going is an unquenchable curiosity about the *intricacies of human nature, and the secrets of human behavior.* These can be fascinating for some people. And if you are one of them, you may be a writer.

We usually did an assignment around this time that produced significant changes in some people's work. The class was to take their small tape recorder and capture some *ad hoc* dialogue out in public. It required a bit of stealth and some daring, but it could be done. They had a week; if their first attempt yielded only "chuffa-chuffa" (writer's talk for lifeless stuff, like the weather) they could do another one, until they got something that had a bit of juice.

Places of opportunity were suggested, like Starbucks, a bus stop, a public restroom. Restaurants are usually not great—too much ambient noise. If the public places yielded *zilch*, or the students lacked nerve, they could set up a dialogue somewhere, even in their own home, and level with the other person about what they were doing, but try to get someone who was in the midst of a divorce or a period of stress or something. The other requirements were to make copies so they could be read in class, and transcribe them exactly as they were recorded with all the "uh's" and "likes" and bad grammar, etc.

Well, when they were read, the class had an epiphany. "So that's the way people talk!"

Yeah, a little different than you've been writing, eh?

During most of the pieces, the rest of the students listened with rapt attention. Their eyes were wide open and you could tell they were following every word. There were lots of laughs too, as opposed to when the students wrote so-called comedy material. The writers would say, "Gee, I didn't think that was funny when it happened."

They learned several lessons: When the actors speak naturally, as they do in life, the audience listens.

Don't forget—these are words created in the person's brain, not memorized from a writer's script. Realistic dialogue holds the attention. Sometimes it makes people laugh just because it's real. If the audience believes they are hearing real dialogue their ears perk up: This is *interesting*!

I would suggest that any aspiring writer try this exercise, not once but many times. I used to do it regularly throughout my career, especially with my kids.

The thing is, listening to actual dialogue gets the audience's interest because they are not listening to words, but *voices*! The best writers write voices. You can hear the characters speak when you read their dialogue. You've heard the expression, "The words jump off the page"? That means when you read the speech of the characters, you can actually *hear what they say*! How do they accomplish this? It's no more than presenting a true expression of what the character *wants* to say in that situation! He may even be lying, but he says what he needs to say to further his self-interest. And you *believe* it! Because it makes absolute sense that this character would say exactly what he says at this point, given the disposition of the person in this situation.

Of course, this takes a good deal of experience with people. Observation and study and living. And interest.

I tell a story about a wedding. It's at the bride's house and the couple is going to spend the first night of their honeymoon upstairs in the girl's bedroom. The party is a rip-roaring affair with much booze being absorbed. Then the newly married pair decides to go upstairs to bed. After a little while, one of the waggish guests suggests that some of them creep up the stairs and cop a peek through the keyhole. They do so, being careful to not make a sound. Two of them, in turn, manage to look through the keyhole and see . . . whatever turns you on. Maybe just the couple sitting on the edge of the bed, smooching. Then a newcomer, climbing the stairs, causes one of the stairs to creak and the couple is alerted, and guesses what is going on. Now they make jokes, for the benefit of the sneaks outside. Rather dirty jokes, I might add.

What happens? Well, for one thing, the mood is broken. The magic is gone. The couple is playing to the audience, and it's just no good anymore. And that's what happens in the theatre. Once the players are aware of the audience, the spell is over and the voyeurs might as well announce themselves and go home. The jokes do not entertain; they only distract.

After the *ad hoc* exercise, we do a scene of the students' invention. Anything goes, as long as they try to remember that the dialogue comes from the volition of the characters. And wonder of wonders, the dialogue sounds pretty real for a change. Instead of hearing the words of real people via the tape recorder, we are now hearing made-up people creating dialogue from the writer's imagination of what the made-up people *want to say*. The students are finally writing!

CLASS EIGHT
CONSTRUCTION

At one point, he said to me, "You avoid the emotional moment."
On a level beyond writing, it applied to my entire life.
I left the class and cried for about an hour. It was a deep
epiphany in a way. It was about much more than writing.
—Marsha Scarbrough,
Contributing Editor/Writer,
Written By Magazine

I'm sure you're aware that not a word has been said about construction. Almost every prospective student that calls about the class says something like this: "I'm not too good with dialogue, but I have great ideas. And I want to learn about construction."

Well, I say nothing, because if I told them the truth, I would lose that student instantly. The truth is, I don't believe in construction. And I know full well, there are writing teachers out there that deal exclusively in construction, and their books make oodles of money. But those teachers generally don't make any considerable amount of money from writing! Except from their books on construction!

See, I believe that storytelling is kind of a natural thing. All of us, from an early age, were pretty good at telling stories, true or false. And we never worried about construction. It always seemed a simple thing to tell a story that was interesting. The main thing was that if the story was interesting to us, it would probably be interesting to other people. And if it was not all that interesting to us, we could diddle with it to make it more interesting. All we had to do was *intensify*—make the hero more avid and the obstacle more obstructive. Give the situation higher octane. The obstacle needn't just be reluctant. He can be actively malignant. And that seems natural, too. Real stories, told by the numbers, always seem to need something. And most famous storytellers exaggerated quite a bit.

Think Mark Twain was 100% truthful?

Shakespeare? George Bernard Shaw? Dickens? *Naw.*

They all had vivid imaginations and used them abundantly!

Now if you think there is a discrepancy between realistic dialogue and amplified stories, get this straight! The characters must behave realistically no matter how outrageous the story. Think of *Planet of the Apes, Wizard of Oz, Jaws, Pulp Fiction,* etc. People love outrageous stories, but insist on believable conduct from the characters.

If you read the rich writing teacher's *How-to* books and believe that on page thirty you must establish the determining moment, and on page sixty accomplish the character change, your story might become just the wee bit mechanical, *nest ce pas*? Maybe that's why these writing gurus never make much money writing creatively.

A young woman is returning home on a flight from Italy. The high spot on her trip was a brief affair with a gondolier in Venice. She is rehearsing the story she will tell her best friend. She is not thinking about the details of the affair, but the way she will relate it to her friend in order to drive the friend into paroxysms of envy.

Let's see . . . the first time she saw the gentleman he was leading a gorgeous woman and her husband into the gondola. His arms were muscular, the golden hair on them shown in the sun. He had a fabulous smile, such beautiful teeth. He flashed a smile at our heroine as she stood on the dock. Right then and there she vowed to seduce him.

She found out his name and reserved his boat for the next day. He took her on a leisurely, fascinating trip around the city. His English was not good but they managed to inform each other of their backgrounds, and tastes, which proved to be similar in all regards. He found a remote spot where a large tree hung over the water, and they kissed. The rest was heavenly. She did a little rewrite and dropped his first customer's husband, and a few other little changes. The trip occurred in the late afternoon, just before dusk, instead of early morning, which was a lot better. And so on. By the time she landed in Chicago, the story was perfect.

The construction evolved from the writer's imagination, calculating what was likely to turn on her audience, and this is the way construction actually works.

The rich construction experts are not so much instructors as critics. They take a successful movie and dissect what the successful writer did. They remind me of wannabe painters who move a canvas chair into the museum and copy the brush strokes of *Whistler's Mother*. I only mention these charlatans to save students' time and money.

But I can hear the readers wailing, "Why doesn't he tell us how to get a job in the business? How to sell a script?" And here I'm going to sound really mystical. In my experience, when you get good enough, meaning someone is willing to pay for your stuff, it all happens like magic. And really, it's not mystical at all. The industry has a giant ear out there, waiting for someone to reach the stage where they can become employable. And when you get there, suddenly people like your writing, and tell you so. You have been discovered. You get an agent, and probably a job.

Advice about schmoozing your way into the business, getting publicity, networking, is all bullshit. The people in the business are too smart for any of that. They've been through it all, and you can't fool them. You've got to keep writing, work on your writing, get to be a keen observer, and buy a tape recorder.

CLASS NINE
STARTING THE SCRIPT

One week I was parking my car and I realized I was running to his house; I was so eager to get to that workshop because it was so much fun. It was exciting.
—Greg Thompson,
Co-Executive Producer,
King of the Hill

O.K., I told you when you first decided to enroll that in the last few sessions we would write a script, and would do it just the way it's done in the business. Of course, the business has changed a bit since I was writing, but essentially it's the same. The process of writing a script follows some pretty well-established lines. The big difference is the advent of writing staffs, headed by show runners. As I said earlier, in the freelance era writers and teams worked directly with the producer and no one else was involved. Except sometimes there was a story editor, but not too often.

Writing a script for a series on TV, which is what most beginning writers do as an entry into the business, and what many of them do their whole career, (as I and my partners did), is a highly specialized job, full of tension and deadlines. A play on Broadway might take years to complete. Likewise a movie script. But a weekly TV show obviously demands that a new script appear every week. It's an agonizing job and sometimes it seems impossible. People get ulcers, divorces, hives, suffer from depression. It is so stressful and demanding that staffs came into being to distribute the pain.

In the freelance era, every show had a stable of writers, several of whom were working on scripts simultaneously. This gave the producer some leeway. If one script was in trouble, he could rush in another that was in better shape. But still, in the best of circumstances, shows "ate" scripts regularly. Which means they were put on the shelf until someone could make them work. Of course, if your scripts provided too many meals, you found yourself out of work pretty soon.

O.K.. We're going to write a spec script. It all starts with "notions."

These are bare-bones ideas, usually a mere phrase that denotes an area for a story. I can remember one, from the series *Gomer Pyle, U.S.M.C.*, that became a script, written by my partner, Sam Bobrick, and me. It was: "Gomer sees a flying saucer."

The idea was to not develop the notion to any extent, but leave it open-ended so the producer, or, in these days, the staff, could pitch in with their own suggestions and flesh out the story. If it was developed too much by the original writer, it closed off too many doors.

I had a phone call. The woman said, "I'm calling for Mr. Reiner. He'd like you to come in Wednesday afternoon, at four o'clock, and bring some notions."

Wow! Carl Reiner was producing *The Dick Van Dyke Show*, and had seen a sketch I'd written for the Writer's Guild Awards Show. What a break!

I was in his office that next Wednesday, ten minutes early. Carl was friendly, and effusive in his admiration of the sketch. He brought out a box of cigars.

"Smoke 'em?" he asked.

"Absolutely. Thanks."

"Like a darkie or a greenie?"

I took the maduro, and he nodded approval, taking one himself. We were getting on famously!

"Well," he said, "what've you got?"

"I didn't bring any notions . . ." Actually, I was out to impress him, whole hog. "I took an idea and worked it out. I've actually got a complete outline."

"O.K.," he nodded, blowing smoke. "Let's hear it."

I read the outline. He listened respectfully. It took about fifteen minutes. When I finished, he said. "It's good. Very funny. Now let's go down to the set and watch them shoot it."

Mystified, I followed him down to the set. There were Mary and Dick, Morey and Rose Marie. And they were rehearsing the story I had brought in, almost word for word! I was stunned, and learned a valuable lesson that day. There was a reason for notions. Lots of smart people were dreaming up stories all the time, and it's not just coincidence when two people come up with the same story at the same time!

O.K. You've done all the exercises. So the final thing is to write a spec script. The odds are long but it can happen, and it *has* happened, that the script comes out well enough to interest an agent. Then the lucky writer or team is off on a career! What I want you to do is first bring in ten to twelve notions . . .

"Shouldn't we pick a show first? That we want to write for?"

By God, you're right! First you've got to pick a show. I'm getting old . . .

They laugh. "That's O.K."

Now, you're clear on what a notion is, right?

"Well . . ."

A notion is a very peculiar beast. And they might even have other names for it now: "ideas, springboards, etc." but they're notions to me. They might be a sentence, or even a phrase, that mentions an area for a story.

"Gomer sees a flying saucer, right?"

Right. And in the case of Gomer Pyle, it was a fertile thought, because he was regarded as something of a goofball, and if he says he saw a UFO he was in for a lot of cynicism, and he would have to defend himself, especially from his Sergeant, and it would lead to scenes.

Remember, a story is told in scenes and a good notion is one that engenders scenes.

A notion is brief. You mustn't tell too much. A notion is a vehicle to get the ball rolling. The notion inspires the other writers to start pitching. If you have a group to work with, you'll find the other writers are coming up with ideas you hadn't thought of. If you're not working with a group, you and your partner can pitch the idea into a story. If you're working alone, best of luck.

You can tell I'm in favor of partnerships, especially in comedy. Comedy writers are a morose bunch and if they spend too much time alone they might melt down into a low gravy.

So, we are going to try an experiment. We are going to team up. There are an odd number of students, but one girl says she has a prospective partner in mind to write with later on, and she might as well start the partnership for this project. So, O.K., we're ready to go. I want you to come in with ten to a dozen notions and use the tape recorder.

CLASS TEN
NOTIONS

I learned something every time I was there. Everything down to the snack break is very much like what it is like to write on a sitcom. What he gives people is room experience that no writer who sits at a desk by himself will ever get.
—Pat Hazel,
Writer/Comedian

The next week they were in with their notions, and we began the process of writing a script. Mike, who is working with Vince, went first.

"George Michael loses his virginity."

What show is this?

Arrested Development.

O.K. Everybody know the show?

"Sure."

I've seen it, but just a couple of times. George Michael is one of the family?

"Right."

How old is he?

"Fourteen or fifteen."

The rest of the class begins offering information about George Michael. He's smart, he has a crush on his cousin who is about his age. They assume the affair is with his cousin but George Michael says no.

This family is sort of hip?

"Yeah . . . in a kind of crazy way . . ."

Right. So they take a sort of permissive view. They don't want to seem uptight. Sex is natural; it was bound to happen some time. The father suggests the kid bring the girl over for dinner. George Michael agrees. She's a great person.

Next day he reports that she doesn't want to come over. She wants them to come to dinner at her house.

How old is this girl?

"About thirty-five."

Thirty-five! Who is she?

"My teacher."

Everybody laughs. I feel we've got a handle on a script.

They go over to dinner and the father falls for her!

The class is laughing and pitching like crazy.

He's not married?

"No, his wife is dead."

Great. It's a struggle between the father and son.

Mike has more notions, and so does Vince, but everyone is captivated by this first one. That's the one they'll work on. I've compressed the pitching somewhat for the sake of holding interest but this is how we got to the nub of the idea.

Which notion do you go with? The one you like, the one that interests you. The one you think would be the most fun to write. If you have the choice, pick the one that turns you on. So, boys, which notion do you want to do?

"The first one," they say in unison.

Great. I think it can work.

"It's a little racy though, isn't it?"

Yeah. So what?

"Can you do something like that on TV?"

You know the biggest mistake beginning writers make?

"No . . ."

They play it safe. They believe that if they show the brass they know all the so-called taboos . . . and observe them, maybe even inventing a few, it makes them seem like they know the ropes and they're ready to be professionals. It's exactly the opposite! Listen, every agent, director and producer has a mountain of scripts on his desk. From friends, relatives and people on the street. They are bored out of their skulls at these white-bread scripts and probably throw them in the basket before they finish the first page. Do you know why? Because they're dull! Pabulum! Pedestrian and dull! They're what are called, "hummers"; they hum along, and put you to sleep. And they're all polite, and clean-as-a-whistle.

If you want to get their attention, you've got to shake them up! Have some guts; push the envelope, shock 'em! Do you understand? Even if your script is a little too hot, it's the easiest thing in the world to run a line through something after they're through laughing at it!

It was Linda's turn, the girl who was writing with someone outside the class. She'd chosen *Two and a Half Men*. Her first notions seemed a little too sitcomy. Then she had one about Alan wanting his son to take piano lessons, and that spurred some interest.

"The teacher is cute and sexy . . ."

"And Charlie is interested."

He tells her he's always wanted to take piano lessons . . . but he's too old now.

"The kid goes out to play but Charlie gets into conversation with the teacher to keep her there for a while . . . and she obviously digs Charlie."

She looks at Charlie's hands and tells him they're beautiful and perfect for the piano. She holds his hands a little longer than necessary.

"And things get personal."

Berta comes in to clean and Charlie introduces her to the teacher. The cleaning woman leaves the room and Charlie finds out more about the young girl.

She's uninhibited, and, in the course of conversation, reveals she's bisexual, and that interests Charlie a lot. He imagines threesomes and other delights. He makes an appointment for a trial piano lesson, to see if learning the piano is possible.

Charlie buys basketball tickets and gives them to Alan and his son to get them out of the house the evening the piano teacher is coming.

The girl arrives to find Charlie alone and the lesson turns into a téte-a-téte with a good deal of wine. They wind up in Charlie's bedroom.

The next morning Charlie wakes up and turns in bed to find Berta looking at him. "She had to go," says Berta.

"Oh," says Charlie.

Berta smiles. "I never do anything like that, but it was nice."

Again, the pitching was compressed a good deal, but you can see the progression.

Jen and her partner, Kevin, were next. They wanted to do a script for *My Name Is Earl*. I winced and explained that several students in my last class had picked that show, and had a great deal of trouble. The MO of the show was ephemeral. It was hard to see any path they were trying to follow. Earl, a former crook, wins the lottery and decides to pay back everyone he has wronged in life, not necessarily with money, but to make up for the offense somehow. I asked the writers if they had another show they could work on, but they wanted to do *Earl*.

The notion that seemed the most promising was one that dealt with his former wife. She had gotten tickets for a concert of her favorite musical group, but Earl had scalped them and pocketed the money. It was difficult to right this particular wrong because the band had split up and any chance to hear them again was slim. The writers were planning to make their story about Earl trying to reassemble the band.

Listen, I said, why not make it that the most important member of the band had retired? That focuses the problem at least. They thought that might work. And, since we were all tired, we left it at that.

CLASS ELEVEN
THE STEP OUTLINE

There are many good writers in this town . . . but there aren't
a lot of good teachers. Bill happens to be both. He knows what
he's talking about and he knows how to explain it to you.
—Rob Lotterstein,
Creator/Executive Producer,
The War at Home

Before we'd broken up the previous week, I had given the students a suggestion for the days ahead: Play with your story. Whenever you have a spare moment—driving your car, sitting on the toilet, whatever, use your imagination. Visualize the situations. Picture the characters. See them in your mind's eye, in scenes that might relate to your story. The scenes do not have to follow in any particular order; it's merely meat on the bones. Next week we'll try to string the scenes together to have the story make sense. That's the second step. It's called the Step Outline. I'll give you a sample outline that resulted in a script next time. Good luck.

The step outline is the heart of the process of writing a script. Once you have a solid step outline, the script is a snap. You have the skeleton; all you do is put some flesh on the bones.

Writing a step outline follows a rather rigid form. In my day it was about three pages. Lately, I've seen examples that were ten pages long, way too much for any sensible purpose. The outline was set up in numbered scenes. These scenes depicted what *happened* in each scene. What *happened*! No dialogue, unless it's essential to the story. No jokes. If a step outline contained a lot of dialogue or jokes, you could be sure the writer was trying to camouflage the fact that he was unsure of the story and trying to bluff it through.

The purpose of the step outline is to make sure the writer and the producer or show runner are on the same page. It validates the agreement on the story. It's like a contract. On many shows the network gets a copy and this is their chance to weigh in if they have any suggestions. It's much easier to change something of the story in a step outline than it is in a script. It's like blueprints for a house. You can change the location of a window or door with a stroke of the pen. Once it's built, it requires major surgery.

The students were assembled. Jen and Kevin seemed to have a lot of notes. So I suggested they go first. Kevin read from the notes. You remember the story: Earl scalped some tickets for a concert his wife wanted to go to, and he is now trying to make amends. However, the band she wanted to hear has now disbanded.

Kevin reads a long description of how Earl tries to reassemble the band. It's dull as dishwater. Listen, I say, I've been thinking about this, and I have a thought. How about having just the main guy resign? Like in The Rolling Stones . . .

"Mick Jagger."

Right. He wants to spend more time with his family. It focuses the problem. There's only one guy you've got to get.

"O.K."

So Earl goes over to the musician's house and meets . . . let's call him Johnny. He looks a bit weary. He has a nice wife, but an eight-year-old boy who's a gangster, a kid from Hell. The kid is rude, belligerent and obviously hates his father.

Everybody laughs.

Right. A nasty kid is funny. The kid talks back, kicks his dad in the shins, throws his toys around. And laughs at his father. Johnny is unbelievably tolerant, can't discipline the kid. He just seems to enjoy his antics. When Earl talks about rejoining the band, Johnny shakes his head. "I'm having too much fun with my family."

Earl goes and sees his ex-wife, tells her of her hero's situation. She says if that snot-nosed kid heard a record of his father, he'd change his mind.

The next day he goes to see Johnny with a record and a small player. They get the kid to come in and Earl plays the record. It is great music and the kid listens intently. But he won't believe it's his dad. "He can't do anything," says the kid. "All he does is lay around. Somebody else played that."

When the kid goes to bed, and his wife goes upstairs, Johnny brings out a bottle. He hasn't had a drink in five years, but he's going to have one now, and asks if Earl will join him. Absolutely, says Earl.

Sometime later they are both smashed and Earl feels he can be frank with the musician. He says gently that he doesn't want to butt into the other man's life, but he can't help noticing that Johnny's kid is a problem.

Johnny breaks down and cries. "I've tried everything," he says, "but the kid has no respect for me."

Again, Earl goes to see his wife. "There's only one thing to do," she says.

"That's what I figured," says Earl.

"But I want to come with you."

"O.K."

They are in Johnny's living room, talking to the musician. Johnny is reluctant. "I don't know if I can do it," he says.

"Of course you can," says Earl. And his wife concurs.

"It's in your blood," she says.

"And I don't know if I can fit into the outfit."

"Sure you can."

Finally he is convinced. He goes out and comes back in a silver jock strap and a black T-shirt, carrying a dusty clarinet. He wipes off the instrument and plays a tentative, abbreviated scale. "I can't," he says.

But Johnny's kid is in the doorway, followed by his mother.

"C'mon in," says Earl. "Your dad is gonna play something for ya'."

"Really, I can't," says Johnny.

Earl's wife gives him a push.

"It's your only chance," says Earl.

Johnny's face is pained, but slowly he brings the clarinet to his lips. And blows. It's hesitant at first but little by little the sound blooms into music, beautiful music. The kid stands there, transfixed.

Finally it ends and the boy goes forward into his father's arms. Johnny stands there, hugging the boy like crazy, tears in his eyes.

"That was great, Dad," says the kid. "Even though you did hit a couple a clinkers."

Linda's story was already worked out and fit pretty well into a step outline. Alan wants his son to take piano lessons. Charlie objects, even though he uses the piano in his job of creating jingles. "I'm not living in a house where a kid is learning the piano," he says. "If he takes piano lessons, you find another place to live and your own piano."

But when the teacher arrives, Charlie changes his mind in a hurry. She is a doll. Charlie says he loves the piano and wishes he could play it better. He even plays a couple of jingles to show off. The teacher is impressed and Charlie feels he is making time with her. When the lesson is over, the kid goes out to play and Alan leaves for an appointment, leaving Charlie alone with the teacher.

She says she feels he has talent and could really play quite well. She examines his hands and says they are lovely and holds them a moment or two longer than necessary. Things get personal. Charlie tells her she is beautiful and probably has many boyfriends. She smiles and says she has close friends of both sexes. Charlie is surprised and asks if she is bisexual. She admits it, freely. Charlie has visions of threesomes and other intriguing things. He makes a date for her to give him a trial piano lesson on Wednesday. You know the rest. He and the piano teacher get a little drunk and wind up in bed. But when Charlie wakes up the next morning he finds he's in bed with Berta. The cleaning woman smiles and says, "I never did that before, but it was nice, no?"

A common mistake that many fledgling writers make is to be too critical. I believe it is done to appear professional. Professionals must be very critical, no?

No. And I'll tell you why. Being extremely critical can cause you to dismiss promising ideas too quickly because they're too far out. Think of the movies that would never have been made if writers had been loathe to play with an idea before giving up on it: *Ghostbusters, Planet of the Apes, War of the Worlds, Groundhog Day* — you get the idea.

Professional writers have an accepting attitude of any notion, at least for a while. You never know when a weird concept can lead to a blockbuster. A goofy thought can develop into a flight of fantasy.

The secret is: The characters must react believably no matter how outrageous the situation. *The Wizard of Oz* held the audience because the cast behaved realistically in the circumstances.

♦ ❖ ♦

Mike and Vince's idea also underwent some changes in this second round of examination, and although the results were a little short on how specific we could be on individual scenes I think we came to a general conclusion on how to make the story more appealing.

George Michael tells his father, after a good deal of reluctance, that he has lost his virginity. The boy is full of guilt but his father has quite a different reaction. As a matter of fact, he immediately gets on the phone and calls several of the older members of his family. They are exclusively male. He asks about their availability for a family dinner.

Two nights later, the dinner takes place and it is rather a fancy affair. All the men are dressed in tuxedos, even George Michael, who has obtained a tux through his father's largesse.

When dinner is over the women are invited to leave so the men can be alone. Now brandy is brought out and a box of cigars, and the men get ready for what is, apparently, a family tradition. With the eldest man present going first, and descending in age, each man recites the story of his own defloration. There are three or four flashbacks to illuminate the occasion, and we were unable to provide exact details of the scenes, but they were presented as a challenge. Research, my boy!

Talk to friends, relatives, read a few romantic books. The result could be a memorable script. And, of course, George Michael's story is the final account. Good luck!

MISCELLANY

A WORD ABOUT CENSORSHIP

Censorshipis something you will have to deal with in various amounts and intensity, depending on the circumstances. If you're working for Disney it's different than HBO. I hate censorship and censors! They introduce an element that interferes with good writing and the presentation of effective drama, comedy, whatever. They always want to cut your best line. If it makes them laugh it must be dirty. And it is always motivated by a childish attempt to establish virtue by compromising reality.

They protest that people are offended by some words. Fuck 'em! It's understandable that people can be offended, but by *words*? War, the needless killing, wounding, mutilation of young people; senseless cruelty, torture, destruction . . . I get it. But words that express human feeling under stress, come on! The biggest mistake that any writer can make is to censor himself. It's like cutting your own balls off. You might have to compromise sometimes—there are plenty of censors out there, eagerly waiting to screw up your work, but for God's sake don't do it to yourself! It's like committing suicide.

FAN SCRIPTS

I first ran into the phenomenon of Fan Scripts when I was twelve years old, working on a radio show in Chicago. The show was called *Vic and Sade* and it ran for a dozen years. It was a unique show and cultivated a large audience. It became almost a cult. Well, after it was on the air for a short time we began getting snippets of scripts and sometimes whole scripts replicating the program. We had no idea of what was motivating these anonymous donors, except that perhaps they enjoyed the show and wanted to participate in some way.

Years later when I got into the writing business, I saw examples of these scripts again, especially as a story editor. But now these scripts seemed to be part of an endeavor to get a job on the particular program and was sort of a spec to show the senders' ability.

These scripts all had a common thrust: They seemed founded on the desire to copy the atmospheres of the show exactly. The characters all echoed their manner of speaking in performance and if the show used catch-phrases of any kind they were sure to be in evidence aplenty.

The scripts presented an odd result: All the *attempts* at authenticity combined to achieve a sort of unreality, as if the show were being done at a wax museum. What was missing completely was the attempt to tell a story, and the effect was as if empty costumes were floating around without bodies in them. And certainly without minds or volition.

In the years to come I saw a lot of these scripts, written mostly by amateurs but from a few professionals as well. I called them "Kinko Scripts" because they seemed determined to present an exact copy of the show they saw last week.

Suffice it to say that "Fan Scripts" will never return a check and that experienced people in the business can recognize them a mile away, though perhaps they have other names for them.

Do not write Fan Scripts!

WORKING WITH A PARTNER OR ON A STAFF

Most comedy writers work in twosomes and there are good reasons for it. The most important, perhaps, is that it is easier to get hired. Employers get two for one—two brains for one check. But that's certainly not all. Other reasons are probably obvious if you think about it. Partnerships are more conducive to comedy—two guys are more apt to noodle with a comedy with a comedy idea than one lonely, morose Jew who can think about little else than paying his rent. Two guys can improvise aloud, stimulating each other into turning over more rocks. They can amuse each other, keep each other pepped up, so that the grim business of writing seems more fun. One writer, working alone, seldom laughs out loud, while two guys, plumbing the edges of a comedy notion, might laugh a lot. And all this leads to more adventurous comedy, even inspirational at times.

But inexperienced writers are often afraid of getting a partner. It can be hard on the ego, sharing the credit. It can be selfishness, not wanting to share the dough. Sometime they've tried it with unpleasant results and they're reluctant to try again. "We just didn't get along," they say. "He didn't understand my sense of humor and I didn't understand his."

Yeah, it can be tough. I remember getting my first partner. His name was Sam Bobrick. He was a tall, gangly, awkward New Yorker who had written jokes for a talk show host. We got together under the auspices of Carl Reiner, who was producing *The Dick Van Dyke Show* at the time. Sam had never sold a script before, while I had sold a couple, which made me the senior guy.

Somehow we got a job, writing a show for Andy Griffith, and set about the job of doing the script. "This has got to be funny," said Sam. "Really funny. It's our one chance. If we blow this, we're in the toilet."

"Thanks for your confidence," I said. Sam didn't even get the barb.

"It's got to be great," he said. "Really funny. Otherwise we'll never get another chance."

"Oh, hell, shut up, will you!" So our partnership was launched.

And dramatic writers partner up too, perhaps not as often as comedy writers, but they do, predicated on the old adage, "Two heads are better than one."

The job of finding a good partner can be as difficult as finding a mate. The ground rules are nebulous. But the main criterion has got to be intelligence. A smart person makes a better partner than a dumb one. Personality is not as important. As a matter of fact, a difference in outlook and attitude can be very effective. I had three partners in my career and I was not fond of any of them. None of them were social buddies. After work was done, I didn't especially want to see them until the next day. But we were held together by the fact that we made money together and actually did some pretty good work.

Sam and I twice won the Writer's Guild Award for the outstanding script of the year in the Comedy category. Though the first time we worked together I thought, "What the hell have I got myself into?" Everything he said sounded weird and amateurish. Then, out of desperation, I decided to listen to him and actually consider what he suggested, and, shockingly, I realized that what he was saying might sound foolish at first blush, but it had promise, with some adjustment, of morphing into an off-beat, delicious bit of humor. Right there I had an epiphany: the weird and unusual can be the doorway to outrageous fun. And we were on our way to some productive, profitable stuff.

My second partner was certainly strange enough. Many people thought he was nuts. He had a sort of Woody Allen personality and, as a matter of fact, looked a lot like Woody. He had never written a script but made his living by hanging around Vegas comics and suggesting bits that fleshed out their routines. Harvey and I, after some time, became producers of some very good shows and had a very successful five years together, but by this time I was willing to listen carefully to him and find the gems in the trash.

My experience working on a staff was limited because I came in on the beginning of the idea of staffs. Up until this time the freelance mode was in force. Writers, alone or in partnerships, sold their ideas for scripts directly to the producer. I think Garry Marshall was the first to employ a staff. Garry had contempt for writers and figured you got jokes if you had more people, quality be damned. So he picked up ambitious young writers, practically off the street, paid them a pittance and started a big operation.

But even with my paucity of experience, I soon saw that the principles of working on a staff were very similar to working with a partner, only multiplied by six or more. You had to go in with an accepting, receptive attitude, go along with anything, but keep alert for any possibility. Don't reject any idea, but investigate it for what I might become. Good ideas came from lowly beginnings. They needed to be mined, twisted, amplified, and adjusted. That was the work of a staff. And I might say that any staff member who rejected ideas out of hand, got personal, declared they say that story last week on another TV show, could expect to be out on his ass in short order. Keep the ball rolling, is the rule.

SUCCESS STORIES

When students have completed the course, they are eligible for the Workshop. This group meets once a week, on Thursday night, and is devoted strictly to professional writing: TV scripts, features, plays, and books are all attacked here. Some of the members of this group have gone on to jobs in the industry, and some of those who are working at the present time come back to sharpen up material of some kind.

Rob Lotterstein and my daughter, Ellen, wrote for numerous shows, including *Dream On, Caroline in the City, Ellen, Boy Meets World, Holding the Baby, Suddenly Susan, Grosse Point,* and *Will and Grace.* They also created the pilot, *Sixteen to Life.* On his own, Rob created the show, *The War at Home.*

Ellen Plummer and her partner, Sherry Bilsing, are Emmy winners for their work as co-executive producers of *Friends.* They have also written for *Veronica's Closet, Joey,* and *Teachers.*

Steve Atinsky has had a novel published, *Tyler on Prime Time,* and has just completed a second book for kids. He and his writing partner, Dan O'Connor, were on the *Payne* staff and wrote scripts for *The Weekenders.* Dan was also the co-creator of the improv show, *World Cup Comedy,* produced by Gramnet.

David Warick and Amy Debartolomeis are a husband-and-wife team whose credits include *Maggie,* and the animated shows, *The Weekenders, Lilo and Stitch,* and *Lloyd in Space.*

Aron Abrams and Greg Thompson were Co-Executive Producers on *King of the Hill* and Consultants on *Everybody Hates Chris.* They have also written on *Fired Up, Maggie, 3rd Rock from the Sun,* and *Grounded for Life.*

Eugene Pack is an Emmy-nominated writer and creator and Executive Producer of the shows, *Signs of Life, Celebrity Autobiographies: In Their Own Words, Dallas Cowboy Cheerleaders: Making the Team,* and *Back to the Grind.*

Michael Jamin's credits include four seasons on *Just Shoot Me* and five seasons on *King of the Hill.*

Aron Abrams & Greg Thompson

Marsha Scarbrough is an accomplished journalist who has written numerous articles for *Written By*, the magazine for the Writers Guild. She is the Writer/Producer/Director of *The Magic of Martial Arts* and award-winning children's DVD and the author of *Medicine Dance: An Adventure into Native American Mind-Body Healing.*

Bill Habeeb is the author of *Inside Mayberry: The Andy Griffith Show Handbook* and has a short story in the recently published collection, *First Times.*

Bill Habeeb

Geoff Tarson and Beth Seriff have written for *Suddenly Susan, That's So Raven,* and *Half and Half.*

Pat Hazel is a comedian and writer who has had multiple *Tonight Show* appearances and created and starred in the TV show, *American Pie.*

David Warick & Amy Debartolomeis

Dennis Haley & Marci Brown

Michael Jamins

Ellen Idelson

Rob Lotterstein

Jeff Lewis

Steve Atinsky

Dennis Haley and Marci Brown are Humantis Prize winners in animation for *Jakers! The Adventures of Piggley Winks*. They have also written numerous episodes of *Clifford the Big Red Dog*.

Jeff Lewis may be the best sketch writer alive and has had his work appear on HBO and in theaters all over town.

These former students and others, who have had exposure to the world of professional writing, drop by occasionally to try out a script or sketch and get some feedback from people they trust.

Ellen Plummer & Sherry Bilsing

Dan O'Connor

Marsha Scarbrough

APPENDIX A

SAMPLE OF A
STEP OUTLINE

This is an outline that became a script for *Get Smart* and won the Writer's Guild Award for Outstanding Script in TV Comedy in 1967.

STEP OUTLINE

"VIVA SMART"
ACT ONE

1. It is evening and Smart and 99 are in Maxwell's apartment. She is ironing his shirts and the atmosphere is very cozy and romantic. The doorbell rings. It is a delivery man from Chile Delight with an order that Max has not called in. Before they can discuss it, the delivery man falls forward into the apartment with a knife in his back. He gasps, "The third tortilla from the bottom," and dies. The tortilla has a hole in it and 99 guesses it is a recording. They play it on the turntable and hear a message from Isabella, daughter of the president of San Saludos, saying her father is being held prisoner and Smart must come rescue him.

2. They are in the Chief's office next day. The Chief tells Smart and 99 that everything has been worked out. The two spies will impersonate José Olé and Conchita, Spanish dancers, who are to appear at the celebration in San Saludos. Once there, they will get Isabella and her father out of prison and bring them back to the U.S. The Chief provides a portable gas balloon and some exploding cigars to aid the rescue.

3. In San Saludos, after a precarious flight, Smart and 99 make their way through customs with some difficulty, because of a suspicious customs office. Smart gives him a cigar in friendship. They encounter one of their agents who tells them that Lopez, their contact, had been hanged that morning.

4. Arriving in the plaza by taxi, they are met by General Sanchez, the villainous officer, who has imprisoned President Hernandez. He welcomes them and declares that his is looking forward to seeing them dance tomorrow. Smart says it is the day *after* tomorrow. No, says Sanchez, they have moved it up because he couldn't wait to see them dance and watch Olé do his famous leap over four horses.

ACT TWO

5. We are in the plaza and it is Fiesta. General Sanchez and Isabella are in a box waiting for the dance of José Olé and Conchita. Sanchez tells Isabella that if she marries him, her father will be released from the dungeon. If not, it's curtains for the old bird. It's time for the famous dance to begin, but Smart and 99 do not appear. After a moment, they are dragged in by soldiers who say they caught the couple trying to escape form a window in the hotel. Smart tries to weasel out of dancing by complaining he has an ingrown toenail, but Sanchez bellows that they'd better begin the dance if they don't want to get blown away by a firing squad. They start dancing and are not doing badly. Smart gets caught up in the thing and begins swinging out, but then the four horses are brought in. The crowd screams for the leap, and Smart tries, but crashes into the side of the first horse. He and 99 are dragged away as impostors.

6. They are in the dungeon—Smart, 99, Isabella and Don Carlos. In the background they can hear the sound of the firing squad. It looks like it's over for the four of them. A guard comes up to the bars and whispers that he can possibly persuade the firing squad to use blanks. Smart is outraged by the show of corruption, but is urged to take the deal by the others. However, Smart

decides to bargain just for the principle of the thing. They haggle back and forth until they are a mere dollar apart, but Smart declares they've had his last offer. He is urged to give in by 99 and finally does, handing over sixty American dollars. The guard goes and is back in a few moments with good and bad news. He was able to bribe only half of the firing squad, but the good news is that Smart gets half his money back, less ten percent for the guard who booked the deal.

7. Smart and the others are facing the firing squad. He tries to delay in vain. The squad is about to shoot. The officer yells, "Ready . . . Aim . . ." Smart yells, "About face!" They do. The officer yells, "Fire!" and they do, killing him.

8. In a field behind the dungeon, the four escapees are standing beneath a gas balloon, which will take them all to safety. However, when they all try to get in they find that the balloon was designed to carry three, not four, since it was not anticipated that Isabella would also be trying to escape. They argue about who will remain behind, each offering to sacrifice himself. Meanwhile, a contingent of soldiers arrives, and it looks like it's all up with our heroes.

TAG

The soldiers stand there with their guns and Don Carlos tells them to shoot and get it over with. But they explain that they have deposed Sanchez and want Don Carlos to be their ruler again.

APPENDIX B
VIVA SMART
BY BILL IDELSON & SAM BOBRICK

This script was written as a result of an arbitration by the Writers' Guild. Sam and I had claimed that Leonard Stern, head of Talent Associates, owed us for two scripts he'd ordered from us on a show that had been canceled before we had a chance to deliver them.

He claimed he didn't owe us anything because we hadn't delivered the scripts. We claimed he was full of shit because we weren't going to hand in scripts for a show that was already canceled and that we would have delivered the scripts if the show had continued, and furthermore, we had passed up other work because we had set aside time to write the scripts he'd ordered.

The Writer's Guild took the matter under advisement, and you must know that Mr. Stern was an influential member of the Guild and had been involved in many high-level activities of the union, so the whole matter was touchy.

Their verdict was that Leonard had to pay us for two scripts, but we had to earn the money by writing the scripts for the ongoing show, *Get Smart*.

This script was the first of the two. The ironic twist was that this script, a first draft by the way, (because they'd butchered our second draft), was nominated for a Writer's Guild Award in the '67-'68 season, and was up against a script written by Stern himself on the same show.

We won. He'd forced us to write a script that beat him out for a Writer's Guild Award. How sweet it was!

GET SMART
"VIVA SMART"

FADE IN:

INT. MAX'S APARTMENT

MAX and 99. Max is sitting on the couch reading a magazine. He is dressed in a smoking jacket and is smoking a cigar. 99 is ironing his shirts. She holds one up.

> **99**
> I just have to do the pajamas and I'll be all finished.

> **MAX**
> I sure appreciate this, 99. Do you know what they want for shirts at the Chinese laundry? Twenty-four cents a piece.

> **99**
> Well, I enjoy spending an evening like this. It's so domestic. It's almost as if we were...well...

> **MAX**
> Twenty-four cents a piece. And they don't even put them on hangers.

Just then the door bell rings.

> **MAX**
> Who can that be? It's almost midnight.

Max goes to the door and opens it. A MAN in white Mexican peon clothes, wearing a sombrero, is at the door with a package of food.

MAX

Yes?

MAN

Maxwell Smart?

MAX

Yes.

MAN

Chile Delight. I have your order.

MAX

Chile Delight? There must be some
mistake. I didn't order anything.

MAN

Take it anyway. It's very good.
Especially the tortillas.

MAX

Don't be silly. With my stomach?
I'd be up all night.

MAN
(looks around)
Take it! Take it! Please!

99

Who is it, Max?

MAX
(turning to her)
Why it's a delivery man from Chile Delight.

99

Oh, Max. How thoughtful. I knew
you'd finally buy me dinner.

> **MAX**
> But this isn't my order, 99. This
> guy made a mistake . . .
>> (he turns toward the man)
> Listen, mister—

There is no one standing there. Max looks down. We see the man crumpled on the floor with a knife in his back.

> **MAX**
> Hey! 99!

99 rushes over.

> **99**
> Max! He's been stabbed!

Max leaps into the hall, looks around.

> **MAX**
> No one out here—

> **99**
> Max, who could have done this to
> him?

> **MAX**
> Well, I'm sure it wasn't a
> satisfied customer. If I were you,
> 99, I wouldn't touch that food.

Max bends over the body.

> **99**
> Is he dead?

The man lifts his head and groans.

MAN

Not yet.

MAX

Who are you? What's all this about?

MAN

Eat first! Talk later.

MAX

Huh?

MAN

The third tortilla from the bottom.

He slumps over dead.

99

He's dead. The poor man.

MAX

Yeah, I wouldn't have his job for a
million dollars.

99

The tortillas!

99 picks up the package of food and searches through it.

MAX

I'll bet they're not hot. They
never deliver hot tortillas.

99 is going through the tortillas.

99

He said the third from the bottom
(she pulls one out)

99

Look, Max. This tortilla has a hole
in it.

MAX

Well, there's no use asking him to
take it back.

99

Max, you know what this is? It's a
recording.

MAX

Why I'll bet you're right, 99.
(takes the record)
Give it here—I'll play it.

Max gets up and goes to his phonograph. 99 follows him.

MAX

I wonder if it's 45 or 33 1/3?

99

It must be 45. Pizzas are usually
33 1/3.

Max puts the tortilla on. We hear a rotten mariachi band.

MAX

That's one of the worst tortillas I
ever heard.

99

Play the other side.

MAX

Right!

He turns the tortilla over.

> **ISABELLA (V.O.)**
> This is the daughter of Don Carlos
> Hernandez, the president of San
> Saludos. My father is being held
> prisoner in a dungeon beneath the
> palace of General Diablo Sanchez,
> an agent of KAOS and an enemy of
> our people.

> **99**
> Why, that's terrible, Max.

> **MAX**
> Yes, but not as bad as the mariachi
> band on the other side.

> **ISABELLA (V.O.)**
> Please, Mr. Smart. You must come to
> San Saludos and save my father
> before he is killed. P.S. Please
> destroy this tortilla after you
> have played it.

> **MAX**
> How do you like that, 99? Don
> Carlos Hernandez of San Saludos a
> prisoner of KAOS. Wait till the
> Chief hears about this. I'll call
> him right now.

He starts off. 99 holds out the tortilla.

> **99**
> Wait, Max. What about this? She
> wanted it destroyed.

MAX
Oh, yes—give it here, 99.

He breaks the tortilla in half and gives one piece to 99.

MAX
Eat first. Call later.

They both start eating the tortilla.

FADE OUT.

ACT ONE

FADE IN:

INT. CHIEF'S OFFICE.

CHIEF, Max and 99. There is a satchel on the desk.

> **CHIEF**
> Now, Max, 99, we've got everything
> worked out for you. Once you get
> through customs, you'll be met by
> our agent down there—*Numero cinco
> y ocho y quatro y seis y nuevo y
> uno y dos.*

> **MAX**
> Gee, that's a long number, Chief.

> **CHIEF**
> They have long numbers down there.
> It's sort of a family number.

> **MAX**
> Oh.

> **CHIEF**
> But you can just call him Lopez.
> When you meet him you'll give him the
> password—Fernando Lamas loves Delores
> Del Rio. He'll take you to the capital.

> **99**
> Fernando Lamas loves Delores Del
> Rio. Right, Chief.

> **CHIEF**
> You will take this satchel with you . . .
> the lining contains 3,000 pesetas.

> ### MAX
> Wow, that's a lotta patatas. How
> did you get 'em all in the satchel?

> ### CHIEF
> Not potatoes, Max. pesetas. That's
> Saludian currency.

> ### MAX
> (relieved)
> Oh, good. A man could hurt himself
> carrying all those patatas . . .

> ### CHIEF
> Now this should be plenty to bribe
> your way into the dungeon . . . and
> get Don Carlos out.

> ### 99
> Right. But after we get him out
> of the dungeon—then what,
> Chief?

> ### CHIEF
> This satchel has a false bottom.
> Look at this.

The Chief presses a button and the bottom falls out.

> ### CHIEF
> It's a collapsible balloon that,
> when filled with special hi-
> expansion gas, is powerful enough
> to safely lift three people. The
> air currents at San Saludos should
> carry all three of you right to
> the coast where we can pick
> you up.

MAX

Great gimmick.

99

Fantastic!

CHIEF

I suggest that as soon as you get into San Saludos you plant the satchel in a field just outside of town, so it will be ready for your escape.

MAX

Got you, Chief.

CHIEF

And one last item . . . these cigars, Max. Each one has the power of a small bomb—in case of emergencies.

MAX

Right.

99

Getting out seems to be all taken care of, but how do we get in? Won't they be suspicious of us?

CHIEF

I've taken care of that too, 99. As you may or may not know, for years Control has been publicizing certain fictitious celebrities just for situations like this.

MAX

I don't get you, Chief.

CHIEF

We've created people, Max. People
that are known all over the world
except that they don't exist. For
instance . . .

The Chief picks up a small poster showing a magician pulling
a rabbit out of his hat. The rabbit covers the magician's face.
On the poster we read:

XANDU THE MAGICIAN
MIRACULOUS MAGIC

CHIEF

Xandu the Magician.

MAX

I've heard of him! He's great.
He does the famous barrel trick.
He puts an elephant in a barrel.

99

And then what?

MAX

What do you mean and then what?
That's the trick. Getting an
elephant in a barrel.

CHIEF

But you've never seen him, have
you, Max?

MAX

Well, now that you mention it,
Chief, no.

CHIEF

Because he doesn't exist. We've
created him. And if you ever do see
him, he'll be one of our agents.

99

That's brilliant, Chief.

CHIEF

And we also have Zubin Rubin and
the Santa Barbara Philharmonic.

The Chief holds up a poster showing the back of a man conducting
a huge orchestra. The poster reads:

ZUBIN RUBIN
ONE NIGHT ONLY

CHIEF

We use him when we have to get a
big group in someplace.

MAX

How do you like that? No Zubin
Rubin.

The Chief holds up a poster of a rock 'n roll group. They are
bearded with long hair. The poster reads:

PAPA GRASS AND THE BANANA SUBMARINE—
THEY'LL FLIP YOU OUT OF YOUR MIND

CHIEF

Papa Grass and the Banana
Submarine.

The Chief holds another poster showing an ice skater spinning.
It is blurred so that you can't make out her face. The poster reads:

THIS WEEK
THRILLS ON ICE
GLORIA DURSHLAG AND HER DANCING SKATES

CHIEF
Gloria Durshlag and her dancing skates.

MAX
I'm dazed, Chief. I hope you're not
going to tell me there's no Debbie
Reynolds.

CHIEF
There are a lot more, but here's the
important ones for you two.

The Chief holds up a poster of two Spanish Flamenco dancers. The man's back is slightly toward us. Both of his hands are held high, covering his face. The girl's whirling dress and long hair cover her face. "José Olé and Conchita. World-Famous Flamenco Dancers. See José do his famous death defying leap over four horses."

99
(reading)
José Olé and Conchita. World-famous
flamenco dancers. See José do his famous
death defying leap over four horses.

MAX
Wow, I'd give anything to see them,
Chief. I flip over flamenco dancers.

CHIEF
Max, you and 99 are going to be
José Olé and Conchita.

MAX
What?

CHIEF

That's right, Max. San Saludos is having a fiesta and we've already booked you as the featured attraction.

MAX

Think of that, 99. We're going to be stars. Listen, Chief. Just out of curiosity, what are they paying us for this?

CHIEF

A thousand pesetas. Less ten percent for Control. After all we did book the deal for you, Max.

MAX

Well, that's fair.

99

But, Chief. Max can't dance. He can't event do the bugaloo. How could he possibly do a flamenco and leap over four horses?

CHIEF

He won't have to, 99. The fiesta is on Thursday. You're scheduled to arrive Wednesday afternoon. You'll make your escape that very night.

MAX

Oh, but what about all those people? Won't they be disappointed? After all, they came to see me, Chief?

CHIEF
(ignores Max)
Your plane leaves in twenty
minutes. You'll fly to Buenos Aires
where you'll make connections with
a local airlines that will bring
you into San Saludos. Max, this is
a difficult assignment and your
lives will be in danger every
moment, but I'm sure everything
will go smoothly if you just
remember one thing.

MAX
What's that, Chief?

CHIEF
While you're down there, don't
drink the water.

DISSOLVE TO:

LOUDSPEAKER

Camera is on CLOSE SHOT of loudspeaker.

SPEAKER
(Spanish accent)
Welcome to San Saludos. All
passengers on the Tequila flight
please line up at Customs to
inspect your luggage.

CAMERA PULLS BACK TO:

EXT. SAN SALUDOS AIRPORT
Customs. A table is set up near the outside of a building. A
sign reads: "El Customs." Two soldiers, a Sergeant and a Private

with a rifle are our customs agents. There are three peasants in the line having their luggage inspected. One has a chicken. We can tell it is not too classy an airlines or airport. Max and 99 step in the end of the line. They are now disguised as José Olé and Conchita. Max has long sideburns and a moustache. 99 has a black wig tied in a bun, very Spanish looking. She has a beauty mark on her cheek, and is now a typical Spanish beauty. They have a suitcase plus the secret satchel.

99

Boy, Max, am I glad that flight is over. I've never been so terrified in a plane in my life. The engine kept missing, the wings kept flapping, and we just missed that mountain . . .

MAX

I wasn't worried for an instant.

99

Really, Max?

MAX

I just kept my eye on the pilot. He was so cool, so calm, so confident . . . just watching him I knew everything was all right.

99

Look, Max. There's the pilot now.

MAX
(calling to him)
Oh, yeah. Hello, Señor Pilot. Splendido flight! Bravo! Excellente! Gracias!

CUT TO:

THEIR POV

The PILOT. He is dressed in old-fashioned pilot's clothing, goggles, leather cap, scarf around the neck, etc. He has a liquor bottle in his hand. He waves happily to Max, takes a swig from his bottle and then gets down on his knees and kisses the ground.

MAX & 99

> **MAX**
> Thank goodness we're going back by balloon.

> **99**
> Do you think we'll have any trouble getting the balloon through customs?

> **MAX**
> Of course not, 99. This false bottom satchel is too clever. They've never seen anything like this.

ANOTHER ANGLE

The line has moved. There is only one man in front of Smart. The man has a satchel exactly like Smart's. The Sergeant has discovered the false bottom.

> **SERGEANT**
> What? Another false bottom suitcase?

SMART

He looks at 99.

ANGLE ON SERGEANT

> **SERGEANT**
> You stupid pig! You think you can
> outsmart us with this foolishness?
> What are you smuggling in here?
> Instant coffee?

> **PEASANT**
> But señor Sergeant! It's caffeine
> free. Real coffee keeps me awake.

> **SERGEANT**
> You'll have no trouble sleeping now.
> Take the dog out and shoot him.

The soldier takes the peasant out.

> **PEASANT**
> No... no.

It's now Max and 99's turn. They hand the Sergeant their passports.

> **SERGEANT**
> Ahhh. The famous José Olé and Conchita.
> You have come to perform at the fiesta?

> **MAX**
> (nervous)
> Yes, we've come to perform at the fiesta.

> **SERGEANT**
> (enraptured)
> José Olé and Conchita! For years I
> have admired you, for years I knew
> of your famous leap over the four
> horses. Tell me, do you still do
> the famous leap over the four horses?

Max puts his luggage on the table.

MAX
Yes, but I've improved on it.

SERGEANT
You have?

He eyes the satchel.

MAX
Now I leap over four horses and a false bottom satchel.

SERGEANT
Ha, ha—you expect me to believe that, señor?

MAX
(low)
No, but listen, Sergeant. We're men of the world. How would you like to earn five hundred pesetas?

SERGEANT
Five hundred patatas? What would I do with five hundred patatas?

MAX
Pesetas! Not patatas.

SERGEANT
Excuse me. I always make that mistake. That's a funny word pesetas. Tell me, señor, are you trying to bribe me?

MAX

In one word: yes, I am.

SERGEANT

Do you know how much five hundred
pesetas is worth? Twenty-five cents
in American money.

MAX

Twenty-five cents? Why, 99, do you
realize the Chief only gave me a
dollar and a half? Boy, he's a fast
guy with a peseta but when it comes
to a few bucks . . .

99

(to Sergeant)
Look, how much do you want to let
us go through?

The Sergeant thinks for a moment.

SERGEANT

A thousand pesetas.

MAX

A thousand pesetas? That's only
fifty cents.

SERGEANT

You're right! Two thousand pesetas.

99

Pay him, Max, pay him.

MAX

Right!

Max opens the satchel and pulls out some bills and gives them to the Sergeant.

> **SERGEANT**
> Thank you.

The Sergeant sees the cigars in Max's suitcase. He takes one out.

> **SERGEANT**
> Wait a moment—What is this?—
> American cigars? Do you mind?

> **MAX**
> Well, ah, ah . . .
> (helpless)
> No. Help yourself.
> But you'll forgive me if I don't
> light it for you. Come on, 99.

They rush off.

SERGEANT

The Sergeant looks after Max and 99 for a moment. He bites off the end of his cigar and spits it out. He then picks up a phone. The Private returns.

> **SERGEANT**
> (on phone)
> Get me General Sanchez.
> (to Private)
> I am calling the General. I have a
> strong suspicion about our last two
> visitors.

The Private strikes a match and brings it toward the Sergeant's cigar.

SERGEANT
Hello, General . . . Listen to this, please...

The cigar is lit. There is an explosion.

EXT. ANOTHER AREA NEARBY

Max and 99 are hurrying. They turn at the blast and look up in the air in the direction of the explosion.

99
Oh, those poor men.

MAX
Don't waste your sympathy on them, 99. They were killers and they would have killed us too if we hadn't given them fifty cents.

99
You're right, Max.

MAX
Now the Chief said after we got through customs we would be met by our agent down here, Lopez. Where do you suppose he is?

99
There's a fellow over there, Max. I wonder if that could be him.

THEIR POV

There is a peon sitting against the wall in the classic tradition of the peasant taking a siesta. A huge sombrero is over his face. Max and 99 walk up to him.

MAX

Lopez—?

LOPEZ
(not looking up)
Si, Señor.

MAX

Fernando Lamas loves Delores Del Rio.

LOPEZ

Oh, Señor. You want Lopez the spy.

99

You are not Lopez the spy?

LOPEZ

No, I am Lopez the Informer.

MAX

Oh. How would you like a cigar, Lopez?

LOPEZ

I know you are Control agents but I will not inform on you if you give me one hundred patatas.

MAX

You mean pesetas.

LOPEZ

No, I mean patatas. I have the french-fry concession at the fiesta.

Max takes some money out of the satchel.

> **MAX**
> Listen, Lopez, I'll give you a hundred pesetas and you can buy the patatas.

Lopez takes the money.

> **LOPEZ**
> Gracias, señor.

> **MAX**
> Now I want some information from you. Where is Lopez the spy?

> **LOPEZ**
> He is hanging around the plaza, señor.

> **99**
> Hanging around the plaza? What's he doing there?

> **LOPEZ**
> Just hanging. They hung him this morning.

> **99**
> Oh, Max, think of that . . .
> *Numero cinco y ocho y quatro y seis y nuevo y uno y dos* is dead.

> **MAX**
> Yeah. Well—I guess his number was up.

LONG SHOT—EXT. PLAZA

It is a very sleepy plaza. There are just a few peons around, all very inactive. A burro cart moves toward the center. In the cart are Max and 99. The burro is being led by the DRIVER, an old man. It stops right in the center of the plaza. The driver pushes down the meter.

> **DRIVER**
> Here you are, Señor, Señorita, the
> heart of town. Just as you wished.

> **99**
> How do you like this, Max? This is
> the Capital of San Saludos.

> **DRIVER**
> (sadly)
> Yes, it has changed a great deal
> since I started driving here. It's
> not the same peaceful little town.
> The hustle, the bustle, the noise,
> the traffic, the smog . . .

> **MAX**
> Smog? You have smog in San Saludos?

> **DRIVER**
> Yes, but General Sanchez is solving
> that problem.

> **99**
> Really? How?

> **DRIVER**
> He is shooting the owner of the
> taco factory this afternoon.

> **MAX**
> Hmmm. How much do we owe you for
> the ride?

DRIVER

Ten pesetas.

MAX

Ten pesetas? All the way from the
airport here? Boy, that's cheap.

DRIVER

You're right. Twenty *pesetas*.

Max hands him some money. The Driver hands the suitcase and
the satchel to Max. Just then a peon with a push cart comes
INTO THE SHOT and stops in front of Max.

SOUVENIR MAN

Souvenirs of San Saludos! Wallets,
bedroom slippers, funny hats,
mellow yellow . . .
(to Smart)
You care to buy a souvenir to
remind you of your glorious visit
to San Saludos, Señor?

MAX

No, thanks. Not right now.

SOUVENIR MAN

(looks around surreptitiously)
Perhaps the señor would be
interested in these.
(he pulls out some
postcards from
his coat and flicks
them quickly)
Art photos.

MAX

Oh? How much?

SOUVENIR MAN

Two pesetas.

MAX

That's reasonable.

SOUVENIR MAN

You're right. Four pesetas.

99

Max, what do you want with those?

MAX

Well, we have to buy something, 99.
After all, the poor man is trying
to make a living.

Max hands the man money and takes the postcards.

MAX

Why! The dirty swindler.

99

What's wrong, Max?

MAX

I've been taken. These really are
art photos. Look, here. The Mona
Lisa, Venus DeMilo, Blue Boy. You
know, it's tricks like this that
give South America a bad name.

ANOTHER ANGLE

GENERAL SANCHEZ is beating his way through a cluster
of several peasants. ISABELLA is behind him. The General
is menacing. Isabella is beautiful.

GENERAL

Out of my way, you filthy peasants!
Dogs, scum of the earth. Out of the
way before I have you shot!

MAX, 99 & DRIVER

99

Who is that?

DRIVER

It's our beloved General Sanchez,
friend and defender of the common
people.

General Sanchez and Isabella come INTO THE SHOT.

GENERAL

Ah . . . Greetings distinguished
visitors to our humble country. You
are the magnificent José Olé and
Conchita.
   (he kisses 99's hand)
I recognized you on sight. I am
General Diablo Sanchez, beloved
leader of the common people.

With his whip, he swings at several peasants who have made the
mistake of coming too close.

GENERAL

Back you pig, you dog! You are
breathing on my boots.

99

It is a pleasure to be here in your
fair country, General Sanchez.

MAX
Yes, it's a real tropical paradise.

GENERAL
Thank you. I try to keep it that
way. Of course at times it is
difficult. We are constantly
beset with spies, foreign agents,
college students, those who would
interfere with our domestic
tranquility.

Suddenly we hear a volley of shots.

99
What was that?

GENERAL
The firing squad taking care of an
enemy of the state. Don't bother
yourself—It happens all the time.
May I present Señorita Isabella
Hernandez, my future bride.

Isabella steps forward and gives her hand to Smart. Smart bends
down to kiss it.

ISABELLA
(whispering)
I am the one who sent you the
tortilla. Did you get it?

MAX
(whispers)
Yes. It was delicious.

Smart steps back.

MAX

I compliment you on the choice of a
bride, General Sanchez.

GENERAL

Thank you. And I compliment you on
the choice of a dance partner, Señor Olé.

99

Thank you.

GENERAL

I cannot tell you how I have looked
forward to seeing your world-famous
performance. I have already
obtained the tallest, most
magnificent horses in my country
for your leap.

MAX
(looks at 99)
Good! Good! The taller the better.
Tomorrow you shall see the
performance of your life.

GENERAL

Tomorrow? You do not dance
tomorrow, Olé. You dance this
afternoon.

MAX

What? *This* afternoon? Wait a
minute . . . The Chief told me . . .

99
(covering up)
Uh—We were under the impression
we would dance tomorrow, General.

GENERAL
Oh, no. The dancing is this
afternoon. The executions are
tomorrow. That's the main purpose
of the fiesta. It's Clean-Up Week
in San Saludos. Come, follow me. I
shall take you to the royal suite
where you shall get ready.

The General turns and starts to beat his way through the peasants.

GENERAL
Away, pigs, dogs . . . scum—

Max and 99 are alone for an instant.

99
Max! Max! What do we do?

MAX
Well, you heard the General. The
schedule is clear. We dance this
afternoon and the executions are
tomorrow.

99
Oh, Max.

FADE OUT.

END OF ACT ONE

Act Two

Fade In

Ext. Plaza

It is set up for the entertainment. There are a few tables, a few people on the ground. On a low platform an act is in progress—two cheap non-union acrobats. General Sanchez and Isabella are sitting in a special little box. Isabella is sad. The General is enjoying himself.

> **General**
> Why are you so sad, my little
> pigeon? In the midst of this
> wonderful fiesta?

> **Isabella**
> You know why I am sad, General.
> My father lies rotting in your
> dungeon.

> **General**
> It won't be for long. Right after
> the wedding we will let him out.

> **Isabella**
> Yes, to be shot by the firing
> squad.

> **General**
> (hurt)
> Isabella, I gave you my word that
> if you married me, no harm would
> come to Don Carlos.

> **Isabella**
> But I do not trust you.

The General shakes his head, reproachfully. The act is over. The people applaud. The M.C. comes on the stage.

M.C.
And now, ladies and gentlemen, the
act you've been waiting for, the
really big attraction of the
fiesta, the world famous, everybody
knows them, José Olé and Conchita.

The people applaud.

GENERAL
Ah, now we shall see something.
Even you, my sad little canary,
should enjoy this.

Sanchez stands up, applauding. All the people look in the direction they expect José Olé and Conchita to come in from. They do not come in.

GENERAL
Where are they? Where are José Olé
and Conchita? Bring them on! Bring
them on!

Just then several soldiers bring on a struggling Max and 99. They are in their costumes.

MAX
Let go of me. Take your hands off
of me.

GENERAL
What is the meaning of this?

1ST SOLDIER
We found them at the rear of the

hotel, General. They were sliding down bedsheets from their hotel window.

GENERAL

Sliding down bedsheets? Why would you do a thing like that, señor?

MAX

Well, it's an old show business custom. A lot of entertainers leave their room that way.

GENERAL

Well, you are here and we are ready for your performance. You are prepared for your leap over the four horses?

MAX

I've been meaning to talk to you about that, General. You see I've got this ingrown toe nail . . .

GENERAL

So?

MAX

Well—would you settle for three chickens and an iguana?

GENERAL

Enough of this nonsense. I am growing impatient. Begin now. No more delay. Escort them to the stage.

The soldiers lead Max and 99 to the stage. The people applaud.

GENERAL
(sitting down, musing)
I wonder if Lopez the Informer was right.

ISABELLA
What do you mean?

GENERAL
He told me these two were impostors, that they are not dancers at all, but Control Agents.

ISABELLA
(worried)
You cannot believe Lopez. You know that.

GENERAL
We shall see what we are to believe. When they dance, I will know.

MAX & 99

They are on the stage. The music starts.

MAX
99, I have a dreadful feeling that this is going to be José Olé's farewell appearance.

99
Max, we can't afford to think negatively.

MAX
You're right, 99. We'll just have to try our best.

Max and 99 go into their dance. 99 carries the ball. With a rose in her teeth, she starts dancing about. She isn't bad at all. The audience gets with her.

> **MAX**
> Hey, not bad. Where did you learn
> that?

> **99**
> We had a Spanish maid.

She continues dancing.

SANCHEZ & ISABELLA

> **ISABELLA**
> They are very good. They cannot be
> impostors.

> **GENERAL**
> Maybe. We shall see.

The music continues. It starts to get to Max. He finds he can hardly control himself and starts clapping and stamping his feet and yelling "¡Olé! ¡Olé!" The audience loves it.

> **MAX**
> (to 99)
> Hey, 99, they love me—

> **99**
> Take it easy, Max. Don't get
> carried away.

> **MAX**
> No, look at them, 99. We're a hit!
> We're a hit! They're eating it up!

Max starts to stamp his feet a little more. Now he starts to carry the ball. He dances around 99, snapping his fingers.

> **99**
> Please, Max . . .

Max is in another world, carried away by it all.

> **MAX**
> Don't bother me, 99. I'm in the
> *mood.*

SANCHEZ & ISABELLA

> **GENERAL**
> The leap! The leap! Bring in the
> horses.

MAX & 99

> **99**
> (terrified)
> Max, they're bringing horses in for
> your leap.

> **MAX**
> Marvelous! Bring 'em up . . .

> **99**
> But Max, you'll be . . .

> **MAX**
> I can do it, 99. I know I can
> do it.

The music continues. The soldiers bring four horses up to the edge of the stage. The audience starts to yell, "The leap! The leap!"

99

Max! Max!

MAX

Out of my way, 99. Here
I go.

Max takes a flying leap into the side of the first horse and falls
down. There is a disappointed noise from the crowd.

99

Oh, Max.

MAX

I wonder if they'd let me have two
out of three.

SANCHEZ & ISABELLA

GENERAL

Seize them! Take them to the
dungeon.

DISSOLVE TO:

INT. DUNGEON

Max, 99 and DON CARLOS. Don Carlos is an old white-haired
man. He sits on a crude bench against the wall.

MAX

I feel terrible, Don Carlos. I
messed this whole thing up.

DON CARLOS

Don't reproach yourself, my son.
You did your best. You were very
brave to come here at all.

99

That's right, Max. You can't
go through life blaming
yourself.

MAX

Who's going through life? We'll be
shot in an hour.

The door to the cell opens and a guard throws Isabella in. They
ad-lib "Isabella." She rushes to her father's arms.

DON CARLOS

Isabella, why are you here?

ISABELLA

Oh, father. I could not let you die
alone so I confessed to General
Sanchez that it was I who sent the
tortilla to Mr. Smart.

99

Oh, Max. This is terrible. Isn't
there anything we can do?

MAX

I don't know . . . Wait a minute, 99.
Of course there's something we can
do. My shoe phone. I'll put in a
call to the Chief. He'll think of
something.

Max removes his shoe and takes out the phone. It's in several
pieces. Wires hang down.

99

Oh, Max.

MAX
You know something? Flamenco
dancing is not the greatest thing
for shoe phones.

We hear the FIRING SQUAD.

99
What was that?

DON CARLOS
The firing squad. Another poor soul
has gone to his reward.

A guard approaches the cell door.

GUARD
(whispers)
Psst! Psst! Señor!

Max approaches the bars.

MAX
(whispers)
Yeah?

GUARD
(whispers)
In just a few minutes you are
scheduled to die.

MAX
Why are you whispering? Everybody
knows it.

GUARD
You do not understand, señor.
Perhaps I can help you. It has been

GUARD (CONTINUED)

sometimes arranged that for a
certain number of American dollars
the firing squad could be persuaded
to use blanks.

MAX

You mean the firing squad can be
bribed? Why that's terrible!
Corrupt! They should be ashamed of
themselves.

99

Max, Max, listen to him. We may be
able to save our lives.

MAX

Right, 99.
      (to guard)
What's the deal?

GUARD

Eighty American dollars, señor.

MAX

Eighty dollars! Are you out of your
mind? I'd rather die first.

99

Max!

MAX

      (to 99)
You have to bargain with 'em, 99.
They expect it. Do you want us to
look like tourists?
      (to guard)
Forty dollars!

GUARD

Seventy!

MAX

Fifty-five!

GUARD

Sixty-three!

MAX

Fifty-nine.

GUARD

Sixty!

MAX

No. You've had my last offer.

GUARD

Señor, we are only a dollar apart.

MAX

I don't care. It's the principle of
the thing.

99

Max!

MAX

Listen, 99. He's trying to take us.
You can get the same deal in Panama
for thirty-nine ninety-five.

We hear the firing squad go off.

MAX

All right, sixty dollars. Will you
take a check?

> **GUARD**
> Cash, señor.

Max reaches in his pocket and takes out some bills and hands them to the guard.

> **GUARD**
> Gracias.

The guard leaves. 99, Don Carlos and Isabella congratulate Max.

> **99**
> Max, you did it!

> **MAX**
> Now listen, everyone. Here's what we do. When the firing squad shoots we'll all fall down and remain motionless until I see that the coast is clear. Then we'll run to that field just west of the Plaza.

> **DON CARLOS**
> But Señor Smart, we will be captured.

> **99**
> No. We have an aerial balloon hidden there that will take us to safety.

> **DON CARLOS**
> We owe you our lives.

The guard approaches.

> **GUARD**
> Psst! Señor!

Max goes over to the guard.

> **MAX**
>
> Back already? That was quick. Did you do it? Did you bribe the guards?

> **GUARD**
>
> Well, yes and no, señor.

> **MAX**
>
> What do you mean, yes and no?

> **GUARD**
>
> I could only bribe half of them.

> **MAX**
>
> Half of them? That's terrible.

> **GUARD**
>
> Well, it's not all bad, señor. You get half your money back. Here. Twenty-seven dollars.

> **MAX**
>
> Twenty-seven? I should get thirty.

> **GUARD**
>
> Well, there's ten percent for me, señor. After all, I booked the deal.

Max sighs.

WIPE TO:

EXT. PIAZA

Max, 99, Don Carlos and Isabella are lined up against the wall. The firing squad is in position. General Sanchez is talking to them.

GENERAL
Well, my friends, we come to the end of the road, eh? You do not know how it grieves me to have to say goodbye to you all . . . especially you, Isabella, my little humming bird. If only you had not chosen to betray me we could have been so happy together.

ISABELLA
I would much rather die than marry you, you pig, you dog, you rotten, filthy swine, you lowlife . . .

MAX
Shh, Isabella, don't make trouble.

GENERAL
Would any of you like a blindfold? A last cigarette?

MAX
No, but do you happen to have an antacid pill? Our last meal was enchiladas and this heartburn is killing me.

GENERAL
Your heartburn will soon be over, señor. I can guarantee that.

DON CARLOS
Sanchez, I have only one thing to

say to you! You can enslave some of
the people all of the time and all
of the people some of the time, but
you cannot enslave all of the
people all of the time!

The General puts both thumbs to his ears, waggles his fingers.

GENERAL
Yeah, yeah, yeah!

MAX
General—do you mind if we say
goodbye to each other?

GENERAL
Why certainly—go ahead.

MAX
Goodbye, 99.

99
Goodbye, Max. Goodbye, Don Carlos.

DON CARLOS
Goodbye, señorita. Goodbye, Mr.
Smart.

MAX
Goodbye, Don Carlos. Goodbye,
Isabella.

99
Goodbye, Isabella. Goodbye, Max.

MAX
Goodbye, 99. Goodbye, General.

GENERAL
Goodbye, Smart. Goodbye, Don Car . . .
(realizes he's been sucked in)
That's enough!

He goes behind the firing squad to give the orders.

GENERAL
Firing squad, attention!

The squad comes to attention.

99
Max, I just want you to know it's
been wonderful knowing you.

MAX
We're not dead yet, 99. Don't give
up hope.

GENERAL
Ready! Aim!

MAX
About face!

The squad turns around, pointing their guns at Sanchez. Sanchez
does not realize this.

GENERAL
Fire!

The firing squad fires. Sanchez drops. There is confusion.

99
Max, that was brilliant!

Max takes 99's hand.

MAX

Come on. Let's get out of here.

Max, 99, Don Carlos and Isabella run off amidst the confusion.

DISSOLVE TO:

EXT. FIELD

Max, 99, Isabella and Don Carlos come to a spot in the field where the Super Satchel is. Max starts to remove the balloon.

MAX

I'll just inflate it and we'll be
off.

Max pulls out the packet, a cylinder of gas and presses a button.

CAMERA ON THE FACES OF DON CARLOS, ISABELLA AND 99 AS THEY WATCH THE BALLOON INFLATE.

We hear the sound of the gas.

DON CARLOS

Ingenious!

ISABELLA

Marvelous!

99

It really works, Max!

MAX IN BALLOON

The balloon is inflated and held down by a rope. All we see is the basket and ropes going up.

> **MAX**
> Come on, get in. We'll get out of
> here.

They all scramble in.

> **99**
> Wait, Max. We can't all go. There's
> four of us. The Chief said the
> balloon will only take three.

> **MAX**
> That's right. Well, you three go.

Max jumps out and starts to cut the rope to release the balloon.

> **MAX**
> I'll stay behind.

99 jumps out.

> **99**
> No, no, Max. If you stay, I stay.

> **MAX**
> (still cutting rope)
> Get back in, 99.

Don Carlos jumps out.

> **DON CARLOS**
> No, no. You three go. I am an old
> man. It makes no difference to me.

> **MAX**
> Don Carlos, get back in. And you
> too, 99.

Isabella jumps out. The balloon is empty.

ISABELLA
No, I will not go without my
father. If he stays, I stay.

MAX
Look, please, will the three of you
get back in there and . . .

The rope snaps. The balloon rises.

DON CARLOS
The balloon!

ISABELLA
It's escaping!

They all watch helplessly as it goes up.

99
(sees something)
Max, look!

They turn. They are surrounded by soldiers, all with leveled
guns. Max groans.

FADE OUT:

END OF ACT TWO

TAG

FADE IN:

EXT. FIELD

Max, 99, Isabella and Don Carlos are surrounded by soldiers with leveled guns.

99
Oh, Max.

She clutches his arm.

MAX
(to soldiers)
Well, what are you waiting for? If you're gonna shoot, shoot. Get it over with.

DON CARLOS
Yes, shoot, but there's just one thing I want to say first. You can shoot all of the people some of the time and some of the people all of the time but you cannot shoot all of the people all of the time.

MAX
Come on, Don Carlos, this is no time for political speeches.

1ST SOLDIER
I think there is some mistake, Don Carlos. We have not come to shoot you. Now that the General is dead, we are free and we want you to come back and take your rightful place as president of San Saludos.

DON CARLOS
What?

ISABELLA
(hugging father)
Oh, father, father.

MAX
What do you think of that, 99?

1ST SOLDIER
The fiestas were much better when
you were in power. This last one . . .
(he turns his thumbs down
and gives it a raspberry)
The soldiers all ad-lib agreement,
"¡Si! ¡Si!" They all turn thumbs down
and give a raspberry.

Don Carlos turns to Smart.

DON CARLOS
Well! I am president again. How can
I ever repay you, Señor Smart? Name
it! Whatever you wish, is yours.

MAX
Well, I hate to seem petty but . . .
(he pulls postcards from his pocket)
. . . could you get me my money back
on these art cards? It's not the
money so much. I just hate to be
played for a sucker.

99 gives Max a look.

FADE OUT.

THE END

APPENDIX C
THE SHOPLIFTERS
BY BILL IDELSON & SAM BOBRICK

In 1944, Squadron 17 of the U.S. Navy Air Corps was in Guam, waiting for a carrier to take us aboard. There was hardly anything to do, except swim in the crystal-clear, blue-green waters down at the beach, eat fresh coconuts and drink 100-proof alcohol that some of the guys had smuggled from God knows where. I spent a lot of time in our Quonset hut, lying on my bunk and dreaming up ideas for comedy sketches.

My favorite was about a nerdy clerk in a department store who dresses as a store dummy to catch shoplifters who had been bedeviling the store.

Flash-forward seventeen years. My brand-new writing partner, (who had never written professionally before), and I, were shivering in the cold in an alley behind Paramount Studios, blocking the rear entrance to the office of Aaron Ruben, producer of *The Andy Griffith Show*, which was number one or two in the TV ratings. I had told Sam, my partner, that I knew where Aaron parked his car in the mornings, and it was a good place to catch him and tell him we had a good idea for his show.

Sam was grouchy. He didn't believe I knew where Aaron parked his car. I told him to shut up and be patient. Behold! Here came Aaron's big Lincoln up the alley and into a spot in the backyard of the house across the way. He got out of the car and started toward his office, frowning at the sight of the two blokes standing in front of his private entrance.

He came up to us. "Yeah?" he said.

"Aaron . . .," I mumbled, "we've got an idea for Barney. We think it's pretty good. Could we have a minute sometime?"

"Eleven o'clock tomorrow morning," he said, and disappeared into his office.

Of course, we were there promptly at eleven. And I broached the idea I'd had on my bunk in Guam. Aaron jumped on it, and began pitching scenes. And right there I learned that Mr. Ruben was probably the best story man I would ever encounter. Sam and I took notes furiously, and in a couple of hours we had enough for a step outline.

When we left the office, Sam said, "Does this mean we got a job?"

"Of course, dummy."

"Well, it's got to be great. This is our chance. We can't blow it. It's got to be real good."

"You're giving me lots of confidence."

"Well, it's got to be great."

"Oh, shut up!"

But the fact is, it *was* pretty great. Great enough to win our first Writers' Guild Award. This is the script.

THE ANDY GRIFFITH SHOW
"THE SHOPLIFTERS"

FADE IN:

EXT. MAIN STREET—DAY

ANDY and BARNEY are seated in the patrol car watching passersby.

> **BARNEY**
> Hi, Mis' Burton . . .

> **ANDY**
> Mis' Burton . . .

> **BARNEY**
> She's a sweet little woman. Never complains. Never once have I heard the tiniest complaint from that woman. You, Andy?

> **ANDY**
> Can't say as I have.
> (pause)
> What's she got to complain of?

> **BARNEY**
> You kidding? *Sam* . . .

Barney puts his hand up to his mouth as if there's a glass in it.

> **BARNEY**
> (continuing)
> Glug, glug, glug. All the time . . .

> **ANDY**
> You don't mean it.

BARNEY
Just don't ever light a match
if he's breathin' your way . . .
Pow!

ANDY
I didn't know that.

BARNEY
Oh, yeah.

Andy shakes his head, then sees another familiar face.

ANDY
Hi, Ed. Ed Rinker . . .

BARNEY
Hi, Ed . . .

ANDY
(smiles)
He's got his hat on.

BARNEY
(nods)
Yeah . . . I noticed that—

ANDY
Probably heard on the radio the
wind might be comin' up.

BARNEY
Y'know—I wouldn't wear one of
those toupees like he's got for a
million dollars . . . Live in terror
of getting caught in a sudden
gust . . . I mean, if it's gonna go,
let it go, that's what I say.

ANDY

Well, he *is* sensitive about it . . . I
mean, there he is in at the barber
shop, every Friday at 3:30 . . .
pretendin' to get his hair cut. And
everybody knows all he gets is a
shave, a shine, and an eyebrow
trim.

BARNEY

If it ever did blow off out on the
street, he'd die of shame. I really
think he would, Andy.

ANDY

Probably right.

Barney's eye catches something and he speaks very low, out of
the side of his mouth.

BARNEY

Hey, Andy . . . Myra Koontz from the
lingerie shop.

ANDY

Oh, yeah. Uh-uh.

Barney shakes his head and smiles to himself. Andy notices.

ANDY

What's the matter?

BARNEY

How ya' mean?

ANDY

You're shaking your head and
smiling funny.

> **BARNEY**
> Was I? Well, I was just thinking
> about Myra—You know, the story
> that's goin' around.

> **ANDY**
> What story's that?

> **BARNEY**
> *You* know . . .

> **ANDY**
> Barney, I really don't. Tell me.

> **BARNEY**
> Well, if you don't know, I'm not
> going to tell you. I mean it's just
> *gossip* . . . And you know how I feel
> about spreading gossip, Andy.

Andy gives him a look.

EXT. WEAVER'S DEPARTMENT STORE

WEAVER, upset, comes out of the store, looks up and down the
street, sees the squad car and waves to Andy and Barney.

CUT TO:

EXT.—SQUAD CAR

> **BARNEY**
> Well, anyway, the story they're
> tellin' about Myra is . . .

> **ANDY**
> Wait a minute. Ben Weaver's waving
> to us, Barn.

> **BARNEY**
> Oh, yeah.
> > (waves)
> Hi, Ben.

> **ANDY**
> Y'know, I don't think that's a
> *friendly* wave. I think he wants us.

> **BARNEY**
> Yeah?

Andy starts the motor and drives out of shot.

CUT TO:

EXT. WEAVER'S DEPARTMENT STORE

Weaver waits impatiently until the squad car drives up. Andy and Barney get out and go up to him.

> **ANDY**
> You want us, Ben?

> **WEAVER**
> Darn right I want you, Sheriff . . . I
> called, but there was no one in
> your office.

> **ANDY**
> No, we been doin' our policin' out
> on the street. What's wrong?

> **WEAVER**
> Plenty! I'm bein' robbed!

Barney is galvanized into action at this.

BARNEY
Robbed! Why didn't you say so right
off? They in there now? Stand
aside, Mr. Weaver.

He struggles to get his gun out of his holster.

WEAVER
No! No! Put that gun away! I'm not
being robbed *now*. I mean it's not
that kind of robbery. I just mean
things are disappearing from the
store.

ANDY
Disappearing? When did you notice
it, Ben?

WEAVER
Just a few minutes ago. I went to
show somebody a silver tea set I
had . . . and it's gone . . . Then I
started to check and there's a *lot*
of things missing.

BARNEY
(hard)
Well, somebody's walking *off* with
the stuff, that's what's happening.

WEAVER
(witheringly)
Do you think I need you to tell me
that? C'mon, let's go inside,
Sheriff.

They start toward the door.

INT. WEAVER'S DEPARTMENT STORE

There are quite a few PEOPLE inside. Andy, Barney and Weaver come in.

> **WEAVER**
> Business's been pretty good lately.
> Been people in from all over.

> **BARNEY**
> Well, put your mind at ease, Mr.
> Weaver. This is just a routine
> police matter.

He speaks low and confidentially out of the side of his mouth.

> **BARNEY**
> (continuing)
> Lock the doors, Andy, and I'll line
> 'em up against the wall.
> (up)
> All right, you folks . . .

Weaver grabs Barney, hisses at him.

> **WEAVER**
> No, no! Don't do that, you fool!
> You want to ruin me?

> **BARNEY**
> What's the matter with you? You
> want us to break this case or don't
> you? And, you better let go of my
> coat. You're interferin' with a
> police officer.

Weaver lets go, turns to Andy appealingly.

WEAVER

Sheriff . . .

ANDY

Uh, Barn, maybe you just better
take it easy for a minute.

Barney nods grimly, brushes off his coat.

WEAVER

This has got to be handled with kid
gloves, Sheriff.

ANDY

Sure, sure it does. Barney was just
eager to help, that's all.

BARNEY

And a fat lot of thanks I got.

ANDY

Barney, why don't you take a little
look around while I talk to Mr.
Weaver here?

BARNEY
(curtly)
All right. If you want to pussyfoot
around about it—that's your
business.

Barney moves off.

ANDY

Ben, how do you know these
items wasn't lifted at night?
Burglary.

> **WEAVER**
> (shrugging)
> Well, I got a night *watchman*, Asa
> Breeney . . .

> **ANDY**
> Old Asa? Hmmm . . .

> **WEAVER**
> What's the matter?

> **ANDY**
> Well, Asa's getting on, ya' know—
> I just hope he ain't dozin' on the
> job.

> **WEAVER**
> Well, there's not much I could do
> about it even if he is.

> **ANDY**
> How come?

> **WEAVER**
> 'Cause Asa happens to be my wife's
> uncle, that's how come.

CUT TO:

INT. COUNTER

A MAN is at a counter or table where some small tools are on
display. He is examining one. Barney sidles up to him and
begins to watch his every move. Man turns and sees Barney's
penetrating gaze, grows uncomfortable, puts item down and
goes away . . . Barney moves on.

SHOT—WEAVER AND ANDY

WEAVER
Andy, these thefts have got to be stopped. What are you gonna do about giving me police protection?

ANDY
Well, we'll certainly be glad to check in here from time to time, Mr. Weaver. Course we can't stay here every minute . . . We're not private detectives.

WEAVER
But I'm being robbed blind.

ANDY
I realize that, Mr. Weaver.

CUT TO:

ANOTHER PART OF STORE

A WOMAN is looking at dresses on a rack, sliding them over as she goes through them. She slides several dresses and finds Barney's face staring at her from the other side of the rack.

WOMAN
Why . . . Barney!

BARNEY
(quietly)
Hello, Mis' Lartz . . . Just go on with what you were doing.

CUT TO:

ANDY AND WEAVER

WEAVER

I pay plenty of taxes for police
protection, you know . . .

ANDY

So does everybody else, Mr. Weaver.
The best thing for you to do is
keep your eyes open, and if you see
anything suspicious, give us a call.
We'll be right over.

WEAVER
(sarcastic)
Maybe you'd like me to get the
crook's name and address, too, to
save you the trouble.

ANDY
(good natured)
Well, that would be a help, I
suppose. We'll have to be goin'
now, Ben.

He turns, raises voice.

ANDY

Barn . . .

PEN COUNTER

Barney has stopped at the pen counter and is examining a pen. He
is so interested in it, he keeps hold of it as he moves toward Andy.

BARNEY

Ever see one of these, Andy? Writes
three colors, got a flashlight,
compass, pocket knife and beer
opener.

ANDY
Let's go, Barney.

BARNEY
(absorbed)
Make a terrific gift for Mother's
Day or . . .

Weaver stands there grimly as Barney starts to leave the store.

WEAVER
Barney! Put that pen back, or give
me a dollar and a quarter.

Barney is startled, turns and looks at Weaver, then goes to put
the pen back.

DISSOLVE TO:

INT. ANDY'S DINING ROOM—NIGHT.

Andy, AUNT BEE and OPIE are around the table, finishing
supper.

AUNT BEE
Well, who in Mayberry would be
stealing from a department store,
for goodness sake?

ANDY
Well, those things have
disappeared. If there wasn't a
little *larceny* in people, there'd
be no need for fellas like me.

OPIE
Maybe it's a gang, Paw. Huh? You
think so?

> **ANDY**
> Yeah, I've thought of it.

He looks at watch, rises.

> **ANDY**
> (continuing)
> I better give Barney a call.

> **AUNT BEE**
> You're not going out?

> **ANDY**
> Yeah. Barney and I ought to do a
> little checking over at the store
> tonight.

> **OPIE**
> Oh, boy!

He slides off his chair and follows Andy over to the phone.

> **ANDY**
> (lifts phone)
> Sarah, get me 427. Thank you.

> **OPIE**
> I'll come with you, Paw, if you
> want me to.

> **ANDY**
> No, Opie. I don't think I do.

> **OPIE**
> But if it's a gang, you'll be
> outnumbered.

> **ANDY**
> (smiles)
> I know.
> (to phone)
> No answer, huh? O.K. Thanks, Sarah.
> (hangs up)
> Must've gone to the movies with
> Thelma Lou.

> **OPIE**
> You better take me, Paw.

Andy goes over and puts on his jacket.

> **ANDY**
> No, I want you to stay right here
> and do your homework.

> **OPIE**
> (disappointed)
> O.K., Paw.

> **AUNT BEE**
> You be careful, now, Andy.

> **ANDY**
> Don't you worry. I'm sure there's
> no danger at all.

He pauses at the door.

> **ANDY**
> (continuing)
> But I might hang around there for a
> while, so don't wait up for me.

> **OPIE**
> I'll wait in the car if you like.

ANDY

No, thanks.

He gives them a reassuring smile and nod and then goes out.

WIPE TO:

INT COURTHOUSE—NIGHT

Barney comes in, goes right to the phone. He has a grim, flat, deadly manner.

BARNEY

Sarah? . . . 596, please.
You got it?

While waiting, he slides gun out of holster, looks at it, drops it back. Takes a bullet out of shirt pocket, breathes on it, shines it on his shirt.

BARNEY

(continuing)
Thelma Lou? Barn here. Yeah . . .
uh . . . this thing tonight, the movie—
I'm afraid it's out, baby.
Well, something big has come up—
police business.
(pause, irritated)
No, *no* . . . it's nothing to do with
trash cans. It's a stake out!
Weaver's store. Well . . . they been
movin' stuff out of there and I got
a hunch they might be back tonight.
Sure, I'm goin' in there alone. I
don't want to bother Andy with it—
he's a family man . . . Well, it's
gotta be done. Just one thing
more . . . In case, uh . . . in case

something happens . . . I want you to
know you're the only one I ever . . .
I ever . . . gave a hoot for . . .
Right. And as far as the movie's
concerned, we'll go tomorrow night.
Yeah, well, keep a good thought . . .
Hm? . . . 'Course I'll be careful.

He hangs up quickly, takes a deep breath, hitches up.

WIPE TO:

INT. WEAVER'S FRONT HALLWAY—NIGHT

Ben is near front door, putting on his coat.

> **WEAVER**
> I'm just going down there and
> find out for myself what sort
> of protection I'm getting at
> night.

> **MRS. WEAVER**
> What for? Uncle Asa's down there
> taking care of everything for you.
> He's a watchman . . . That's what he's
> there for.

> **WEAVER**
> (grunts)
> Yeah. You know what they call him
> around town? Rip Van Winkle
> Breeney.

> **MRS. WEAVER**
> (coldly)
> Are you saying you think he sleeps
> on the job?

> **WEAVER**
> (sarcastic)
> Well, I don't know, Rita, but he
> always looks very well-rested in
> the mornings.

> **MRS. WEAVER**
> Why don't you call in the FBI? Have
> *them* keep an eye on that *junk*
> you've got in stock.

> **WEAVER**
> Junk is it? That junk is keepin' up
> a pretty good house for you.

> **MRS. WEAVER**
> It's junk.

> **WEAVER**
> Yeah . . . well, it still needs
> somebody to watch over it, and I
> doubt if your Uncle Asa's doing
> it.

> **MRS. WEAVER**
> (as he goes)
> It's all junk, that's what it is . . .
> junk!

WIPE TO:

INT. FURNITURE DEPARTMENT OF WEAVER'S STORE

ASA is preparing to have his dinner. He is comfortably set up at display dining room table. He take his limp sandwich and salt shaker out of lunch box and begins eating.

DISSOLVE TO:

EXT. REAR OF WEAVER'S STORE—NIGHT

Weaver comes quietly up to the back door, takes out his keys and lets himself in.

INT. REAR OF STORE

As he comes through door, closes door carefully, but does not lock it. Creeps toward front of store.

FURNITURE DEPARTMENT

Asa has finished his dinner, and is sleepy. Puts elbow on table, cheek against hand, and closes eyes.

ANOTHER ANGLE

Showing Weaver stealing up into position where he can observe Asa. He see Asa snoozing and frowns.

CUT TO:

EXT. REAR OF STORE

As Barney comes up with flashlight. He flashes light at windows.

INT. STORE

Weaver is about to descend on Asa, but suddenly sees beam of flashlight moving around on ceiling, and he ducks down, scared, thinking it is burglars.

EXT. REAR OF STORE

Barney is giving the joint a routine security check. Windows are O.K. He tries the door, opens and closes it, then does a take. The door is open! He opens it cautiously a crack and peers in.

Int. Furniture Department

Asa is sound asleep. His left hand slides off table and knocks salt shaker off. He does not awaken.

Int. Rear of Store

As Barney hears SOUND. He creeps in, gun at the ready. Closes door carefully, then with trembling hand he reaches into shirt pocket and removes bullet. He tries to load gun, but his hand is so tense the bullet squirts from between his fingers like a pumpkin seed and rolls into store. Barney grimaces and crawls after it.

Weaver

He hears these SOUNDS from the rear of store. On all fours he crawls to one side to outflank the burglar.

Barney

He reaches under counter to retrieve bullet. It comes up all covered with lint.

BARNEY
Darn it.

He brushes bullet off, blows on it, rubs it against shirt. Loads gun . . . he peers over counter across store.

Barney's POV

On other side of store, a floor lamp sways back and forth.

Barney

He knows where the crook is now. Crawls to his right and bumps head against packing case.

STATIONERY COUNTER—WEAVER

He rises up carefully, puts hand onto typewriter. Carriage slides across and BELL RINGS. He ducks down.

TOY DEPT.—BARNEY

Crawling with head turned toward sound, puts hand on roller skate and goes flat on face.

SPORTING GOODS—WEAVER

Takes bat off rack as weapon. Crawls.

DOLL COUNTER—BARNEY

Barney rises up to take a look, gun in hand. Peers between dolls. Seeing nothing, he goes down again . . . Barney's gun sight catches in ring of Chatty Cathy Doll. It pulls string out. Barney disentangles gun. Releases string.

> DOLL
> (metallic voice)
> I love you.

Barney clamps hand over doll's mouth.

> DOLL
> Will you play with me?

Barney puts hands around doll's neck.

> DOLL
> You be Daddy and I'll be
> Mommy.

Barney begins pistol-whipping doll.

BARNEY
Shut up! Shut up!

SEVERAL SHOTS OF WEAVER CRAWLING, BARNEY CRAWLING, PEERING AROUND

Barney crawls and finds himself facing a pair of legs. Barrel of rifle is pointing right at Barney's head. Barney realizes he has come to the end of the line.

BARNEY
(low)
O.K. O.K. You got the drop on me . . .

He lets go of his gun and starts to put his hands up, looking up as he does so . . . Sees it is a dummy, dressed in hunting jacket, holding gun. He is furious. Grabs gun again and begins crawling.

INTERSECTION OF AISLES

Barney and Weaver crawl right into each other. Both gasp and leap back before they recognize each other.

SHOTS OF WEAVER AND BARNEY

Crawling in opposite directions, frantically.

INT. REAR DOOR.

It is being opened slowly. Flashlight plays around store.

SHOTS OF WEAVER AND BARNEY

Both stop and turn, terrified that crooks are getting reinforcements.

SPORTING GOODS

Weaver knocks over a bag of golf clubs.

TOY DEPT.

Barney upsets a box of ping-pong balls.

FURNITURE DEPARTMENT

Asa leaps up, confused.

ASA
Who's there? Who's there?

He fumbles, pulls out gun, steps in wastepaper basket, cocks gun and it falls to pieces.

BARNEY

Flat on his face, terrified.

BARNEY
(shouting)
You're all under arrest! I got ya' covered!

ANOTHER ANGLE—WIDE SHOT

As lights go on. Andy is standing by light switch. Weaver rises slowly from behind counter.

WEAVER
Don't shoot, don't shoot . . . It's
me, Ben Weaver.

He sees Andy.

WEAVER
Sheriff, thank goodness it's you . . .
They're all over the place.

ANDY
Yeah? Where? Where?

Barney comes up slowly.

BARNEY
All right, all right, don't anybody
move a muscle!
(tough)
Finally got here, eh, Andy? I been
standing off the whole gang single
handed.

ANDY
What gang?

They all look around.

WEAVER
You mean there's nobody here but
us?

ANDY
Looks that way.

He looks at Barney and Weaver standing there, trembling.

ANDY
(continuing)
Lucky you two fellas didn't meet
each other. Somebody mighta' got
hurt.

Asa stands there, blinking.

ASA
Oh, it's you fellas, huh? I thought
it might be crooks.

WEAVER
(furiously)
You . . . You old fool! There was
enough going on in here to wake the
dead and you slept through the
whole thing!

ASA
Who you callin' an old fool? You
want me to tell Rita?

Weaver growls in annoyance.

WEAVER
Well, I guess this proves you were
right, Sheriff. I probably *was*
robbed during the night. It's easy
enough—with Rip Van Winkle here
on guard.

ANDY
Hold on now, Ben, I don't think it
proves that at all. Actually it
proves just the opposite.

WEAVER
What do you mean?

BARNEY
Yeah, what's your theory, Andy?

ANDY
My theory is—the things that
were stolen had to be taken during
the daytime—during business hours.

WEAVER
Yeah?

ANDY

It's very simple—You said there
was a dozen or so things missing.
Well, if the crooks come here at
night they wouldna' stopped at that.
They'd of moved out the whole
store!

BARNEY

By golly, Andy, I think you're
right.

ASA

(smugly)

Sure, he's right. See, Ben, it
don't happen at night when I'm
here. It happens during the day
when you're here.

Weaver whirls on him and fixes him with an enraged eye.

WEAVER

Asa . . . I've got just one thing to
say to you. You're . . . f . . .

ASA

(quickly)

Don't you do it . . . don't you do it.
Because if you do, I'll tell Rita.
Then you'll be sorry.

Weaver turns away from him, disgusted.

WEAVER

(to Andy)

So that's it, is it? Shoplifters?

Andy

Mr. Weaver, you're bein' robbed
blind in broad daylight.

Weaver

(shaking head)

I'll be dogged.

He starts toward rear of store. Andy and Barney follow him. Asa
stands there until the SOUND of the door closing comes from
rear of store. The he gives a mighty stretch and yawn, settles on
bed in furniture department and goes to sleep.

Fade Out.

End of Act One

ACT TWO

FADE IN:

INT. COURTHOUSE—DAY

Barney is pacing, deep in thought. The door opens and Andy comes in.

> **ANDY**
> Morning, Barn.

Barney does not answer. Andy goes toward his desk.

> **ANDY**
> (continuing)
> *Morning*, Barn.

> **BARNEY**
> Oh. Morning, Andy.

> **ANDY**
> You look like a man with a thought.

> **BARNEY**
> I got more than that, I got a
> theory.

> **ANDY**
> Oh, yeah? What about?

> **BARNEY**
> About who's been doing all the
> stealing from Weaver's store.

> **ANDY**
> Really?

> **BARNEY**
> You want to hear my theory?

> **ANDY**
> 'Course I do.

> **BARNEY**
> It's not pretty.

Andy shrugs.

> **BARNEY**
> (continuing)
> As a matter of fact, it may come as
> quite a shock.

Andy shrugs again.

> **BARNEY**
> (continuing)
> You ready to hear my theory?

> **ANDY**
> I'm braced.

> **BARNEY**
> All right, we'll play it question
> and answer. I'll ask the questions
> and you answer yes or no. O.K.?

> **ANDY**
> O.K.

> **BARNEY**
> All right, here we go: *A*—whose
> store is being robbed?

ANDY

Uh . . . no?

BARNEY

What d'ya mean, *no?*

ANDY

Well, you said answer yes or no.

BARNEY

I meant *one word*. Answer in one word.

ANDY

Oh. Well, you didn't say that.

Barney takes a breath, starts over again, quietly.

BARNEY

All right, we'll start over again from the beginning, and you answer in one word. *A*—whose store is being robbed?

ANDY

Weaver's.

BARNEY

Right. *B*—who's going to collect the insurance on those thefts?

ANDY

Well, Weaver, I suppose.

BARNEY

Right, right . . . *C*—who was creeping around that store last night?

ANDY

You were.

BARNEY
(outraged)
What d'ya mean, *I* were?

ANDY

Well, you *were*, Barn. 'Course I
know that's two words.

BARNEY

Don't be purposely *obtuse,* Andy.
The *answer* is *Weaver.*

ANDY

Well, I missed it.

BARNEY

Well, play the *game*, play the *game*!
I hate when you get obtuse. All
right, where'd I leave off?

ANDY

C.

BARNEY

O.K. *D*—Who in their entire life
got a bargain in Weaver's store?

ANDY
(pause)
Weaver?

BARNEY
(beside himself)
Oh, for gosh sakes! I'm trying to
give you the name of the criminal

BARNEY (CONTINUED)
and you won't accept it! The
answer is *Nobody*!

ANDY
Nobody is the criminal?

Barney halts, glares at Andy.

BARNEY
Boy, when you get obtuse.

ANDY
I'm sorry, but really, I just don't
get what you're aimin' at.

BARNEY
(quietly)
Alright, then I'll spell it out
for you. Weaver is stealing from
his own store himself.

ANDY
What? Weaver? Oh, now—

BARNEY
For the insurance. Don't you see,
Andy—he spirits those things out
of the store, collects on the
insurance, then sells the merchandise,
besides. He gets double on everything.
Listen, I'll bet if we cased the pawnshops
in Silver City, we'd find most of that
stuff.

ANDY
Barney, that's just plain
ridiculous. Ben Weaver's no crook.

A sharp businessman, maybe, but he
wouldn't *steal*. Why, he's one of
the most respected men in town—
one of our best church-going members.
He knows every hymn in the book.

BARNEY

That's a front. You watch him
sometime when we're singing:
"Leaning on the Everlasting Arms."
He don't know the words. Just moves
his lips.

ANDY
(firmly)
Well, notwithstanding, your theory
about Weaver stealing from
himself's plain *hogwash*.

BARNEY
(pause)
All right, you want to hear another theory?

ANDY
No.

BARNEY
Asa . . .

ANDY
Barney!

BARNEY
All right . . . All right.

ANDY
Listen, what we're looking for is a
common, ordinary *shoplifter.*

He glances at the clock.

> ANDY
> (continuing)
> And by the way, the store'll be
> opening in about fifteen minutes.
> Why don't you get over there—
> make Ben feel he's getting a little
> cooperation from us.

> BARNEY
> (shrugs)
> Well, if that's the way you want
> it.

> ANDY
> It is. Just make yourself as
> inconspicuous as possible and keep
> your eyes open. I'll be over and
> relieve you a bit.

Barney is moving toward the door.

> BARNEY
> Could I take just one look into the
> trunk of Weaver's car?

> ANDY
> Barney . . .

> BARNEY
> O.K. O.K.

He goes out.

DISSOLVE TO:

INT. WEAVER'S STORE—DAY

There are a number of people already in the store. Weaver, at the register is busy with a couple of customers, ringing up their purchases. Andy enters.

> ANDY
>
> Morning, Ben.

> WEAVER
> (looking up)
> Oh . . . Morning, Sheriff.

> ANDY
>
> Uh . . . everything all right?

> WEAVER
>
> Far as I know . . . been keepin' my
> eyes open.

> ANDY
>
> Where's Barney?

> WEAVER
>
> Barney? How should I know.

> ANDY
>
> Ain't he here? I sent him over
> about an hour ago.

> WEAVER
>
> Well, I ain't seen him.

Ben goes back to taking care of customers. Andy shakes his head in perplexity, moves into store.

ANOTHER ANGLE

Andy move among the people, smiles and nods to several, but also keeping his eyes open . . . He passes clothing dummy. It is

Barney, who has hunting coat and hat on over regular clothes.

> **BARNEY**
> (clenched teeth)
> Psst, psst, Andy . . .

Andy looks around, bewildered, finally looks at dummy, can't believe it.

> **ANDY**
> Barney!

> **BARNEY**
> (clenched teeth)
> Shh, keep your voice down. And
> don't look at me . . . Act natural.
> But stand by . . . I got my eye on our
> bird right now.

Andy, dazed, forces himself to turn away.

> **ANDY**
> You have? You mean the
> shoplifter?

> **BARNEY**
> Check. Just keep moving . . . Wait
> for my signal.

> **ANDY**
> But Barney, don't you think—

> **BARNEY**
> Just go—go—will you?

> **ANDY**
> Yeah . . . O.K.

Andy moves off, puzzled.

SHOT OF BARNEY

His eyes dart around, to pick up a suspect.

WIDER SHOT

MAN comes up, smoking an evil-looking corn-cob pipe, pauses to examine something close to Barney. Let's out a great cloud of smoke that rises into Barney's face . . . Barney almost gags, starts to sneeze. Forced to move hand dummy-fashion and get finger under nose.

ANOTHER ANGLE

Andy moves slowly up an aisle. LEON comes along with a large sandwich, offers a bite to Andy.

> **ANDY**
> Oh—No, thank you, Leon.

Leon moves on. CAMERA PANS him over to Barney. Leon stops in front of Barney, looks at him. Barney tries to ignore him, but Leon just stands there.

> **BARNEY**
> (clenched teeth)
> Scram . . . Scram, Leon.

Leon raises sandwich toward Barney.

> **BARNEY**
> (continuing)
> No, Leon . . . Uh-uh.

Leon just stands there, holding up sandwich.

> **BARNEY**
> (hisses)
> Please, Leon . . . I'm on a case!

A WOMAN going by, stops, notices Barney, touches COMPANION.

> **WOMAN**
> Say, isn't that Barney Fife?

> **WOMAN #2**
> Where? Oh, you mean the dummy?
> (laughs)
> Say, it does look like him, doesn't
> it? Except that dummy's better
> looking.

Several other PEOPLE stop, look, AD-LIB among themselves, giggle. Barney rolls eyes heavenward.

> **BARNEY**
> (groans)
> Oh, my . . . Now, look what you've
> done, Leon . . . you little . . .

Weaver comes up.

> **WEAVER**
> What's the matter here? Is
> something wrong?

He looks at dummy, his mouth drops open.

> **WEAVER**
> (continuing)
> Barney!

Barney throws up his hands.

> **BARNEY**
> Oh, for gosh sakes! If you'd've
> only waited a coupla more
> minutes . . . Well, I'll have to make
> my move *now*.

He steps off platform.

> **BARNEY**
> (continuing)
> Follow me.
> (calls)
> Andy!

He rushes off.

ANOTHER ANGLE

As Barney comes up fast and grabs a little old LADY with a
shopping bag.

> **BARNEY**
> All right, sweetheart, the game's
> up. This is the end of the line for
> you.

> **LADY**
> What? What? What's the meaning of
> this?

Weaver comes up.

> **WEAVER**
> Barney . . . what are you doing?

> **BARNEY**
> Nabbing your shoplifter, that's
> what I'm doing.

LADY
Shoplifter? Are you accusing me of—
Why of all the nerve. How dare
you!!

Andy comes up close to Barney as woman continues to protest
in B.G.

ANDY
(low)
Barney . . . are you sure? Dead sure?

BARNEY
Stake my reputation as a police
officer. Never saw her before. A
stranger in town. She's the one.

Several people have gathered and are looking on curiously.

ANDY
Uh . . . Folks, would you move on,
please? This is a private matter.

Reluctantly, they break up and move on. Andy turns back and
takes the little old lady gently by the arm.

ANDY
(continuing)
Madam, would you mind stepping over
here?

He draws her off to one side into a corner, Weaver and Barney
follow along.

BARNEY
Just take one look in her bag,
Andy. That'll do it.

LADY

What are you talking about, young man? Are you out of your mind?

BARNEY
(tough)
The bag, sweetheart. Empty it out.

ANDY

Barney, maybe you better . . .

BARNEY

Hold off, Andy, I know how to handle dames like this. The bag, baby, the bag.

LADY

You mean you want to see what I have in my bag?

BARNEY
(heavily patient)
That's right, sweetheart.

ANDY

Actually, madam, you don't have to show us.

LADY

I know I don't, but I'll show you anyway—just to prove how stupid you are.

She reaches in and takes out the two items in it.

LADY
(continuing)
See, this is all I have. My

LADY (CONTINUED)
knitting and this . . . I always carry
this with me wherever I go.

BARNEY
(swallows)
A Bible?

The three men stand and look at one another for a moment.
Barney takes bag, turns it upside down. It is empty.

WEAVER
(dangerously)
Barney . . .

ANDY
Uh . . . Wait a minute, Ben.

He turns to the old lady.

ANDY
(continuing)
Ma'am, I'm afraid we've made a
terrible mistake . . . Y'see, Mr.
Weaver here has been troubled with
shoplifting and my deputy . . .

LADY
Your deputy is a stupid fool.

WEAVER
It was ridiculous. Absolutely
ridiculous . . . I'm sorry as I can
be . . .

LADY
Well, that's not good enough.

Weaver glares at Barney.

> **WEAVER**
> I only hope you'll forgive us . . .
> Here . . .

He reaches over and takes a pen from the table.

> **WEAVER**
> (unctuously)
> Kindly accept this as a little
> gift.

> **LADY**
> I don't want that silly pen—

> **WEAVER**
> Please, madam, just continue
> your shopping. I promise you
> nothing like this will ever happen
> again.

> **LADY**
> What I *should* do is sue you. Sue
> you for every penny you've got.

> **WEAVER**
> Oh, please, ma'am, forgive us—
> you know how everyone makes
> mistakes.

He turns to Andy.

> **WEAVER**
> (continuing)
> Sheriff, you better get him out of
> here before I . . .

> ANDY
> Yes . . . sure, Mr. Weaver . . . Come on,
> Barney.

> BARNEY
> But I saw her—I actually saw
> her, Andy.

> ANDY
> Forget it, Barn—Come on—

Barney continues to protest as they move toward door, Andy trying to calm him.

CUT TO:

EXT. WEAVER'S STORE (FRONT)

As Andy and Barney come out.

> BARNEY
> I saw her just as plain as I see
> you. I couldn't've been wrong, I
> just couldn't've.

> ANDY
> Just take it easy, Barn . . .

Weaver comes rushing to the door, sticks his head out.

> WEAVER
> Barney! Come back here with that
> jacket and hat!

> BARNEY
> Hm? Oh, yeah.

He takes off clothes and gives them to Weaver, who jerks them away and into store.

> **BARNEY**
> (angrily)
> Well, I was just tryin' to help you
> is all.

Barney comes back to Andy and they move slowly toward squad car.

> **ANDY**
> You made a couple of mistakes back
> there, Barney. In the first place,
> you got to be awful, awful, careful
> of who you accuse of shoplifting . . .

> **BARNEY**
> But Andy, when you see 'em with
> your own eyes? How much more
> careful can you be?

> **ANDY**
> And in the second place, you must
> never make your arrest inside the
> store. See, no matter what a person
> has on 'em inside the store, they
> can always claim they were gonna
> pay for it.

> **BARNEY**
> Yeah, but what's that got to do
> with . . .

> **ANDY**
> But when they get *outside* . . . If
> they got something they don't have
> a sales slip for . . .

BARNEY

Andy, would you please postpone the
lecture for some other time? I'd
just like to get out of here right now.

ANDY

No, I don't want to go just yet.
See, I got a little line on a
suspect myself.

BARNEY

Huh? You got a suspect? Who is it?
He inside the store?

Andy glances back, shakes his head.

ANDY
(pause)
No, just comin' out . . .
(quietly)
There's our man, Barney.

Barney looks, is flabbergasted.

BARNEY

Huh?

EXT. FRONT OF STORE

Andy, followed by Barney, comes up quickly, puts his hand on
shoulder of same little old lady.

ANDY
Uh . . . one moment, Ma'am . . .

LADY
(turns, annoyed)
What? Oh . . . you again?

ANDY
That's right.
>(aside)
Barney, go inside and get one of
them bathroom scales, will you?

BARNEY
Bathroom scales?

ANDY
Yeah. *Now*! Get it!

BARNEY
Oh . . . O.K.

He goes.

LADY
>(testily)
You want me to empty my bag again?

ANDY
No ma'am. That won't be necessary.

Weaver comes running out of the store.

WEAVER
Sheriff, for goodness sakes, what
are you doing? Don't tell me you're
annoying this poor woman again?

LADY
Yes, he is. And I'm getting tired of it,
too. This time, I *am* going to sue.

WEAVER
>(low)
Let her go, Andy . . . let her go.

LADY

Mr. Weaver, when I get through with
you, you'll be sorry about this for
the rest of your life.

WEAVER

See? Please, Andy . . .

ANDY

You just hold on now, Mr. Weaver.

Barney comes up with scale.

ANDY

Put it right down here, Barney. All
right, Ma'am, would you step up on
it, please!

She protests but Andy leads her gently onto the scale . . . The
three men look down. Weaver and Barney are astonished.

WEAVER

A hundred and eighty pounds?

BARNEY

(whistle admiringly)
She must be solid. I'm only a
hundred and thirty-two myself.

ANDY

I just can't believe it's flesh and
bones that's making up all that
poundage, Ma'am. Are you sure there
ain't a few other items you want to
tell us about?

BARNEY

Hey . . . it's the *loot*. That's what's

making her so heavy. She's got the
loot on her.

WEAVER
(bewildered)
But where? You opened her bag,
didn't you? If it's not in her bag,
where is it?

Andy gently opens he coat. Many items are hanging from hooks inside. Weaver and Barney look at this display with open mouths.

BARNEY
Will you look at that—a
traveling pawnshop.
(giddily)
See? See? I told you she was the
one, didn't I? I saw her with my
own eyes. See? See? I had her
cold.

The old lady gives Barney a contemptuous look.

WEAVER
But Andy, how did you know? What
tipped you off?

ANDY
I'll tell you, Mr. Weaver—when I
put my hand on her arm inside
there, she clanked. And little old
ladies ought never to clank.

Barney takes hold of the little old lady and leads her to squad car, Andy following close in rear. Barney opens rear door briskly and ushers her inside, then turns and speaks low to Andy, who is right close beside him.

BARNEY

But, Andy, you knew, didn't you?
You knew she was the one right from
the start. Why didn't ya' say
something?

ANDY
(low)
Well, Barney, we'd of blown the
whole thing. If she'd of been sure
we knew she'd of ditched the stuff
before she came out.

BARNEY

Oh . . . oh . . . sure . . .

He leans in to her, sneering.

BARNEY
(continuing)
Well, sister . . . you thought you
were being real smart in there,
didn't you? Thought you really had
us over a barrel. Actually we were
just giving you enough rope to hang
yourself. Think that over! Try and
put one over on the law, huh? Let's
go, and . . .

ANDY

Uh . . . you forget to take your gun
this morning?

BARNEY

Huh?

ANDY

Your gun . . . your gun.

Barney looks down at empty holster, then turns furiously on woman.

Barney

Awright! Hand it over! Hand it
over!

She starts to hand it over as we:

Fade Out.

Tag

Fade In:

Int. Courthouse—Day

Andy is seated at desk. Barney is standing, putting a couple of lumps of sugar into his coffee.

> **Barney**
> Andy, you know what I credit the
> solving of the Weaver case to?

> **Andy**
> No. What?

> **Barney**
> My incredible eyesight. It's really
> sort of fantastic for a man of my
> age, but my eyes are better than
> any kid's. I've got hawk's eyes. I
> can spot a fly clear across the street.

> **Andy**
> I'll be darned.

> **Barney**
> Besides that I've got a
> photographic mind. Anything I see,
> sticks. One look and it's right there
> for me to examine at my leisure.

> **Andy**
> That's astounding.

> **Barney**
> It ain't astounding . . . It's just
> superior powers of observation.

ANDY

Hm . . .

BARNEY

I'm very observant. You want me to
show you? Look, I'll turn my head
and take one *flash* look at that
cell. Then you ask me any question
you want about it. O.K.?

ANDY

O.K.

Barney turns his head quickly, turns it back.

BARNEY

All right, I've got it. It's there
for all time. Ask me something,
about anything in the cell.

ANDY

All right. Where's the floor lamp?
East or West wall?

For an instant Barney looks stricken, then desperately guesses.

BARNEY

Uh . . . East . . . I mean West.

ANDY

East is right.

BARNEY

Sure. See, didn't I tell you?

ANDY

Astounding.

Barney reaches for sugar, then stops.

> **BARNEY**
> Say, Andy did I put sugar in my
> coffee, or didn't I?

> **ANDY**
> Why don't you look at the
> photograph in your mind?

> **BARNEY**
> What? Oh. Oh, sure . . . No, I didn't
> take any.

He takes a couple more lumps, puts it in coffee, stirs it, smiles at Andy, who smiles back, then he takes a sip, makes a slight face.

> **ANDY**
> What's the matter. Not too sweet,
> is it?

> **BARNEY**
> No, of course not. It's perfect.
> Just the way I like it.
> (grimaces)

FADE OUT.

THE END

ABOUT THE AUTHOR

BILL IDELSON is recognizable to fans of *The Dick Van Dyke Show* as Herman Glimpsher, the mother-dominated boyfriend of Sally Rogers (Rose Marie). Long before he played that television role, he was a fixture on radio as Rush on *Vic and Sade*. But to Hollywood insiders, it was his skills as a comedy writer that made him so distinctive. His scripts for *The Andy Griffith Show, The Twilight Zone, Get Smart, The Bob Newhart Show, The Odd Couple* and *M*A*S*H* have contributed to the classic status of those programs. Bill Idelson shared his knowledge of comedy by tutoring a new generation of successful television writers. On the last day of 2007 Mr. Idelson died at the age of 88. Fortunately, he left us with several books: *The Story of Vic and Sade*, a World War II memoir, *Gibby*, a how-to guide, *Writing for Dough*, and the present volume, *Bill Idelson's Writing Class*. His influence will live on.

CPSIA information can be obtained
at www.ICGtesting.com
Printed in the USA
BVHW091944300121
599169BV00002B/403